Dirt, **TRUTH**, Music, and Bungee Cords

Dirt, **TRUTH**, Music, and Bungee Cords

CONVERSATIONS WITH THE SOULS WHO GUIDE MY LIFE

Bud Megargee

Copyright © 2015 Bud Megargee
All rights reserved.
ISBN: 1506091172
ISBN 13: 9781506091174

Imagine sitting across from someone who knows you better than you know yourself: What questions would you ask, knowing you would get the most truthful answers but that the cost would be your truthful answers to the other person's questions in return?

Contents

	Author's Note	xi
	Introduction	xiii
Chapter 1	Who Is Laz?	1
Chapter 2	Laz, Why Me?	11
Chapter 3	My First Spiritual Beatdown	17
Chapter 4	Getting a Spiritual Makeover	48
Chapter 5	A Question of Personal Power	73
Chapter 6	Checking In on Elias	88
Chapter 7	Symbols	91
Chapter 8	Cocreation through Smudging	96
Chapter 9	Relationships, Bungee Cords, and Married Women	105
Chapter 10	On Saving Lives	120

Chapter 11	Communicating with the Inanimate	124
Chapter 12	Consultation on Addiction	128
Chapter 13	The Asylum	135
Chapter 14	Where Do Guides Rest?	140
Chapter 15	Remembering Maurin Pesta	143
Chapter 16	A Peek at the Future	146
Chapter 17	Truth, Dirt, Music, and Angels	151
Chapter 18	Feedback from Laz	158
Chapter 19	Changing Emotional Healing:	164
Chapter 20	Faith, Hope, and Belief	170
Chapter 21	What Laz and Ucerous Really Think	177
Chapter 22	Broken-Glass Souls	182
Chapter 23	Describing the World Where Laz Lives	187
Chapter 24	It's a Pumpkin's Life	194
	Conclusion	201
	Topics from Kadecious	209
	Acknowledgments	211
	About the Author	213

Truth is possible only if I trust in myself and what I believe. Some of my central truths reside within the core of who I am, and to clearly understand what they are requires serious self-examination. If I trust in myself, I can find truth in you, I can find truth in other people, and I can trust the purpose of my existence. But if I don't trust in myself, truth is impossible.

"In one truth lies all truth. If you understand one truth, you understand all truths."

—Thich Nhat Hanh

Author's Note

It is with a great deal of thought and consultation that I have written about my continuing six-year adventure in discovering the truth and purpose of this life and my existence. As you will read, it has been an unconventional path.

During this time I have encountered a spiritual teacher, a number of soul guides and a group of Taiwanese monks, all of whom made some contribution to this writing. It is with their permission, and at their behest, that the conversations you are about to read are presented. Their only request is that I let others know that there are souls who guide us and are available for our personal aid and comfort.

Before we start, my thanks to all the guides and monks who have contributed to these dialogues, all of which have been transcribed as spoken without correction for grammar.

Finally, I thank you for your willingness to take this journey with me. As you will see, what they say has meaning for us all.

Introduction

I have always considered myself to be conservative, sometimes excessively controlling, and certainly overanalytical, but I have consistently been willing to entertain any idea in pursuit of answers to life's problems. *Cautious* and *traditional* would have been good adjectives to describe my existence… until an early fall evening in Maryland several years ago.

It was the evening before I was to appear in court in Northern Virginia to initiate my divorce proceedings. As I watched the clock flip past three in the morning, I knew sleep was out of the question. Each time my eyes drifted open over the course of the night, I looked toward the ceiling, where a strange image appeared no more than three or four feet in front of my face. It resembled a window no more than forty-eight inches square.

Looking through the square was like looking through water, wavy and unclear. I wasn't shocked by it; I was intrigued and wanted to figure out what it was and why it was appearing to me now. The figure stayed for some time, never advancing more than a few feet despite its shimmering movement. As time passed, I began to think that perhaps the message was that I was not thinking clearly; after all, the impending court hearing was not going to be a picnic. I was glad it wasn't a voice speaking to me, just an intense feeling or instinct. As the moments passed, I resolved that this must relate to the court proceeding and that perhaps I was going to be taken to the cleaners. It turned out I was right about that one.

With some hesitation, I now mention one remaining, peculiar portion of the event. I had one steady thought while the window was present. I kept hearing the name Elias in my mind, and I imagined a tall, slender, dark-skinned man, almost Somalian looking. The name had no immediate association in my life, and besides, the window was weird enough. So I dropped all of it and tried to prepare for the probable court outcome, assuming that the stress of the divorce was playing tricks with my psyche.

After the event, I made only one mention of all of this to my daughter, Case. Like most young college students, she found her father's situation amusing. Later that year, however, that would change for her.

Not too long after, I received a panicked call from Case. She was waiting to check into Dulles Airport on a student excursion to Costa Rica, so I assumed she was calling about her recently developed fear of flying. But that wasn't it. She wanted me to describe what Elias looked like; I had not described that to her earlier. When I told her what I remembered, she let out a scream. "Dad, I just saw him out front, and I can see him from here!"

I was puzzled. The District of Columbia is an international community, and this was surely a coincidence; besides, I was convinced that her anxiety over flying had gotten the best of her. I suggested this to Case.

"No," she replied. "He came up to me, told me his name was Elias, assured and comforted me that the flights were going to be safe." She quickly got off the phone, apparently hoping to catch him outside and ask him about the window I had seen. But when she arrived out front with her friend, he was nowhere to be found.

This was my introduction to the world of the souls that guide us. Elias was my first, and I later learned that he had been trying to communicate with me for some time. He has never contacted me again. Perhaps his intention was to begin the process of introducing me to his world and the others who would later touch my life. I often refer to him now as my "introduction guide."

From those moments forward, my life and many of my interests slowly changed. I stayed in my chosen field of mental health, convinced that participating in the construction of healing environments was part of my passion and calling. There was a difference, however—transforming how the healing process takes place became my new focus. I didn't know at the time that I was experiencing my own transformation.

My search for answers about my life's path started as I tried to resolve the message in the window while I lay in bed in Maryland. Despite my best efforts, I just couldn't shake the image. During the hazy moments before sleep when my mind would become quiet, or at various times during meditation, unanswered questions about the purpose of the window image would unavoidability surface. With this persistent picture of the framed window, it was becoming apparent that the message was not just regarding the divorce proceedings; I was gradually realizing that I did not see most things clearly, especially regarding my own personal development.

Despite my best efforts, the glazed window refused to leave my mind. I moved to Virginia, where I sought answers by studying with the Taiwanese monks at Wat Yarnna Rangsee through Vipassana meditation. They taught me to use my insights to fuel the investigation into life's unanswered questions, including the impression of the window. The Buddhist teachers took great patience to share the benefits of meditation, mindfulness, and simple awareness, and at the time it was a welcomed relief that calmed my inner conflicts. The monastery abbot would echo the Buddha proverb, "Jittam dantam sukha vaham"—the trained mind brings happiness—but I needed much more. This gentle monk's emphasis on self-transformation through self-observation only partly answered my difficulties. I wanted to know about the image and to understand the reasons for failed relationships as well as the increasing level of discontent I was feeling with the mental health healing profession and, of course, the meaning behind that damn window. Thai monks from Wat Yarnna Rangsee focused on my inner resolutions to life's challenges but also indicated that there were individuals available to everyone; these individuals had gifts that could not be explained, and, if those gifts were needed, perhaps I would find them...or they would find me.

I was certain that something was missing, and my determination to find reasonable explanations brought me to Pennsylvania, both for work and to live. There I relied on one very close friend who had traveled an unconventional path in her own life. She had become aware of an extraordinarily honest, and insightful individual with psychic abilities and suggested that perhaps a spiritual connection might assist me in finding some of the answers I sought. This oracle, she suggested, was a person considered to be a source of wise counsel and prophetic opinions. So, after some thought and hesitation, I contacted this rare person, who was residing along with her family in northern Pennsylvania. Initially I was a skeptic, but there was one way this individual could become instantly credible to me. I had a picture of a family member and thought that if she could ascertain my connection to the picture, then I might be convinced she could be the resource the Thai monks were referring to. During my first meeting, I surprised this oracle with psychic skills by presenting the photo of a family member, and I was shocked when she stated emphatically that there was no silver cord connecting me with the person in the picture and therefore the person could not possibly be a family member. In fact she was right; I had no biological connection to the individual in the picture, a detail that for most of my life I had kept to myself. The oracle, Shirlet Enama, was totally accurate. Over time I learned that I was not alone in starting my voyage with the talents of this individual. Government officials, Wall Street executives, Hollywood celebrities, and other nationally recognized psychics have sought her assistance, yet always with a veil of secrecy. I would learn the reasons for this high degree of privacy over the course of the next six years and it centered on her access to all the worlds of spirits including those who choose to guide us.

As I entered this unconventional world, I learned from soul guides that the oracle Shirlet was apparently a very old soul who had a gift currently reserved for only seven living humans. When I questioned what this meant, guides who presented early in the dialogues, explained that there were many psychic-like individuals with a wide variety of legitimate skills but very few who could see and communicate with all spirits regardless of their dimension of origin or the energy and vibration level that they revealed. She resides in a very rural community because that is the location given by her own guides, and all the soul guides whom I have encountered speak through her. She doesn't channel them in a traditional sense; rather, she acts more as a translator during our conversations. She does not change voices or become possessed; instead, she tries to rapidly interpret their messages with the same level of seriousness or humor with which they are delivered. She has had this gift since she was a very young child living in California.

What follows is a compilation of my discussions with two soul guides. I share this with the permission of the guides involved and with the understanding that they only want to let us know that they are real and available to all of us for assistance and are eager for us to connect with them.

INTRODUCTION

Above all else, they are truthful, and they take every question literally. As an example, if you ask, "Where am I in this life?" they might respond, "Sitting in the chair in the living room."

They can be humorous, they often speak in allegories, and they are not shy about giving me tasks to complete in order to make a point. They are not psychics and will not give information that would retard my soul path development. When I have worked with these soul guides, they focus only on me and my continued progress, regardless of what I may have accomplished in this life. They have no interest in any individual other than how that person affects me and my soul advancement.

The highly evolved guides I encountered were extremely challenging, especially when they focused on improvement in my soul track. Early on I made the mistake of asking a sophisticated guide named Hamlin to give me a life-development grade; he gave me a minus two and stated that the task of constructing my life was to achieve a ten, so quickly I was taught to be careful what I asked for.

There are soul guides who are very highly advanced, like Hamlin, who might exist to explore the upper levels of our soul advancement, and then there are those who are very, very close to us in this life, serving in a protective fashion. I refer to them as "primary soul guides." Some might see them as guardians, and perhaps that is where the term "guardian angel" comes from. You are about to meet two of mine: Laz and Ucerous, or U.

The encounters with my soul guides were lengthy, and, as you will see, it was a bumpy ride at times. I was not always aware of or prepared for the issues they wanted to discuss, and maybe that was by design on their part. Honesty and truthfulness, at a deeply personal soul level, are their only interests, and I hope that comes across in the dialogue that follows. Again, their intention is to have us know that they exist and that they are regularly trying to connect with us...all we need to do is listen.

CHAPTER 1

Who Is Laz?

When I was attempting to solve some of my unanswered life questions, seeking solutions through personal, private introspection just made me more confused, so I welcomed an alternative. It was never my intention to experience or investigate soul guides; that was not an agenda I sought, and at the time I didn't really know much about soul guides or if I had one. And now, as I pause to consider all the unusual beliefs I have embraced as a result of my six-year adventure, it seems all too offbeat to find myself even writing about them.

I've always wondered why the events of my life seemed to happen for reasons that I could not explain, always when least expected. "All things happen for a reason," friends would say. I had days when that made sense, yet I had been questioning how my thoughts about those events seemed to blend together over time to form a completed puzzle. For example, why in such a short period of time had I traveled from Virginia to Maryland and finally to Pennsylvania to find myself sitting in a room with this oracle? What was the purpose behind that?

One of the reasons for my consistent overanalyzing of life events is that I have a distrustful nature when it comes to situations I can't explain through my professional training. I seem to emotionally tumble while struggling to gain control of those issues. The net result is that I wonder if I am optimistic about finding solutions to personal problems yet skeptical, or in doubt, about how I arrived at a particular conclusion. "Maybe you are a hopeful believer," friends would say. All of them could not have been more wrong.

DIRT, TRUTH, MUSIC AND BUNGEE CORDS

My initial meetings with Shirlet were exploratory and concentrated on the most recent emotional events in my life. I felt that targeting my personal and professional relationships would be fertile ground for any psychic talent. To her credit she was always patient with my repetitive examination of my life dealings and at times would even encourage revisiting a specific failed personal relationship from my time in Maryland. It was only after a number of these recurring discussions that the first soul guide made its presence. It wasn't planned, and Shirlet was as surprised as I was. "Oh, that is interesting," I remember her saying. "You have a guest." I awkwardly fumbled through the largest portion of that evening, and I'll admit that my first response was to freak out. He was extremely challenging, and I was caught off guard. To be honest, I felt foolish. With my control issues, I had to find my balance, a reasonable starting point, if I was to ever continue in this type of undertaking. So after the first chance meeting, I sought refuge in the keeper of all information--the Internet. Entering that world was almost as disturbing as meeting the guides themselves.

Based on what I found, I put together a series of questions to ask a soul guide, such as: "What is your relationship to me?" "Do you have a name?" and more. Armed with the list, I felt prepared should any soul guide choose to interact with me during my time with Shirlet. For her part, Shirlet never advised me one way or another on how to act or what to say. She would only indicate that they were present. Her demeanor was always constant. "If they are here, Bud, you should ask them anything you want to know, and they will never lie to you."

Little did I know that the questions I had so carefully constructed from my Internet search would be viewed by soul guides as completely superficial and would only increase the intensity of the guides' attention to my soul's path. Believe me—they would answer any frivolous question I asked, but then they'd get back to the task at hand, which always focused on the advancement of my soul development.

After months of repeating the same relationship topics with Shirlet, I soon learned that my initial soul guides, as well as others with complex personalities, were determined to change the unproductive pattern I was on and set straight the course for my continued self-evaluation.

Other than the previously mentioned Elias, the first soul guide who interacted with me had a name that Shirlet was unable to pronounce. Determined to complete my list of guide names, I kept at it until he reluctantly agreed to a name. He said, "You can call me John." So from that time on we referred to him as "You can call me John." He was available for only a couple of hours, but I remember being at an emotional loss during most of our conversations. Why? He hammered home the importance of truth, honesty, and humility, none of which fit my initial intention for visiting with Shirlet that evening, which was to discover the reasons for the conflicts in my past interpersonal relationships.

Subsequent chance meetings during these early periods included the appearance of a number of strong guide personalities, all of whom seemed to be softening the beaches for more specific soul-guide interventions. The guide Hamlin appeared only once. I had cautiously decided that exploring soul guides might be of interest to me, so I voluntarily requested more involvement from them. This soul personality was directive and very challenging. I had asked for the presence of a guide, and he accommodated my wish and wanted to know exactly what I needed. My planned inquiries were of no use to me with Hamlin. He would have nothing to do with my shallow questioning, and I remember Shirlet being completely exhausted after his exit. His presence was that of a courtroom judge, without being critical or pejorative. He formulated his questions in such a way that anything other than authenticity was impossible. When I asked about Hamlin's physical appearance, Shirlet responded that all she could say was that he did not present in a physical form but that his voice was that of thunder. There are times I wonder whether he will return and if he has a more significant role for me later; he was very quick to give me a life grade, and although soul guides do not get disappointed, he clearly expected more.

Kadecious was a multifaceted guide who entered our discussions sometime after Hamlin, and he was laden with very complicated questions, several of which are listed at the end of this work. I refer to Kadecious as a "process starter" because his questioning altered my focus, and he dared me to face myself. In a brief task to discover the colors of the rainbow, he illustrated to me how closed my world had become. I was to collect an item for one color of the rainbow every day for seven consecutive days. For example, on day one I collected a red button from my home. After collecting an item for all seven colors of the rainbow, I was to meditate on what I had discovered about myself. My learning? Rarely do I make myself vulnerable and venture outside a well-defined comfort zone. In collecting the seven objects, I had not gone beyond my home or workplace, nor had I exposed myself to any risk. He coined the phrase "No time for doubt" to me, a phrase that would later become the foundation for my continued adventure with all soul guides.

Finally, there was Lazadonton, or Laz as I called him. He was a unique soul guide from the beginning of our association; with him, not only were the dialogues different, as you will read, but the energy and feeling in the room were completely unique. The air in the room seemed to become richer, almost lighter, and there was a feeling of familiarity or inner calm about everything, including me. Both Shirlet and I smiled constantly while he was with us, and Shirlet was especially fond of him and appreciated his candor and his relentless sense of humor. Laz told me that he was not only my protector but that he was always with me, which made him stand apart from the other guides.

After going through my list of questions from the Internet, I asked Laz if there was ever a time when we had been together in a previous lifetime, since I had read that such an occurrence can be one criterion for a soul guide. He indicated that we had been together only once but that he knew me very well, perhaps better than I knew myself. I asked him for details of our common lifetime. He jokingly told me that we had been together in Jerusalem, where we made waffles together. Later I learned he meant bread.

Laz told me that during the life we had together, there had been times when authorities tried to apprehend us. We all laughed because apparently we were mischievous and not always behaving on the up and up. At the end of our time together, as we had tried to flee, I had been unable to outrun the Roman horses or dive along the side of the road, as he could, and had died as a result of an infection caused by Roman arrows. Perhaps as a result of this story, a bond was created between Laz and me; there was certainly something different about him, and I felt it during every encounter. So who is Laz? He is not only my primary protector soul guide, but, as you will learn, he is much more.

One winter evening while visiting northern Pennsylvania, I was curious about the attachment that I felt with this soul guide Laz, and I was determined to learn more.

>Bud: [*to Shirlet*] Is Laz physically presenting this evening? I mean, can you see him?

>Shirlet: All I see are his sandals.

>B: [*joking*] I once asked to see his sandals.

Laz didn't hesitate and jumped right into the conversation.

>Laz: Did you like them? I got them at Foot Locker. [*laughing*]

>B: Sorry, I really didn't see them, nor can I see them now.

>L: [*with emphasis*] We used to make them all the time together. It was something that we did together.

>B: We did together?

>L: [*with surprise*] Yes, together.

>B: Laz, you once told me that we lived together in Jerusalem, right?

>L: [*again with emphasis*] Yes.

>B: I was under the impression that we were poor.

>L: Yes, but you were good at making bread. And sometimes stealing it. [*kidding*]

>B: What were we, poor beggars, street waifs, and nomads?

L: We went from house to house and offered our services for food and shelter.

B: We were handymen?

L: Yes, you were handy with the women. [*laughing*] It works well if their husbands are not in town. It was a bonus to get into a good bed for the night; however, usually they came back, and that is when we were running. [*laughing*]

I am increasingly intrigued with the discussion. Shirlet was eyeing me and shaking her head, hoping that I would get more serious, but I was determined to find out just what my connection with this soul guide was and why I felt it so strongly. It was like having a conversation with my brother.

B: Laz, how old were we? If I didn't live very long, I assume that we were much younger.

L: We were not old. Just in our twentieth years. You died young. You were sick. Shot with an arrow. Infection, sick and died.

B: Were you with me when that happened?

L: Yes.

B: [*looking for a firmer answer*] What were we, street buddies?

S: His tone just changed. He is looking at you very seriously, almost shocked.

L: You don't know?

B: [*looking to Shirlet*] No.

S: He just got really weird, Bud.

B: [*fishing*] Were we related, Laz? [*pause*] Were we brothers?

L: Yes! [*loud and with emphasis*]

B: [*apologizing*] I did not know. I'm here in this shell and…

L: How do you think I know you so well?

B: Sorry, I'm learning about that, and it is so rare that we have discussions like this and that you answer these types of questions so readily. [*pressing the issue*] Were you my older brother?

L: I was older. But you were good at running though.

B: Where were our parents?

L: They didn't live. Don't you remember?

B: No. Is there anyone else in my life now that was part of that life experience with us?

L: Only Shirlet.

S: [*laughing*] How did I get into this? I wasn't doing anything today. I was just sitting here.

B: [*smiling at Shirlet but pressing on*] What was she?

L: She was an oracle that helped us. She eased your pain while you were dying.

I was unaware of any connection prior to this, although I must say that it made sense. Higher guides had informed me previously that there was a purpose in my finding this oracle. Connections from previous lives, I have learned, are not uncommon.

L: [*to Shirlet*] They stoned you to death and killed you. You were young too.

S: Perfect. That figures. [*smiling*]

B: Was it the Roman guards?

L: It was the townspeople. They would get into a frenzy and say that the animals were dying and they were hungry and there was no rain for the crops. They pointed someone out, and they would kill them.

B: Did all this take place in Jerusalem?

L: We traveled everywhere. Both of us did.

S: Isn't that something?

B: Laz, was that your only incarnation here?

L: No, just with you, for now.

B: So you had others after Jerusalem?

L: Yes, but I haven't incarnated lately.

B: I am assuming that you have been with me as a guide for some time and possibly multiple lives—is that accurate?

L: Yes, I have. Trying to help you.

B: [*trying to put all the pieces together, to Shirlet*] He mentioned another guide previously and referred to him as U.

S: Ucerous. He calls him U.

B: [*to Shirlei*] I am getting a very strong feeling right now that Laz and I are together over there, the same cluster of souls, same area...

L: If you don't spiritually develop, we won't be together when you pass.

Apparently my guess was right. Laz and I were of the same group when I was in spirit, and I assumed with this comment that my delayed spiritual development is a cause of concern. I have learned that souls develop whether incarnated or not, and Laz was suggesting that I am not keeping pace.

B: So we have been together?

L: Yes, but now you must develop.

S: Bud, he is trying to keep the two of you together.

There were times when subjects would change rapidly and I would feel like I was on the game show Jeopardy. I would get information only if I formulated the proper question, and Laz only gave me an answer to the question—not much more. I came to understand that sometimes the message came in the form of feelings or intuition. Here is an example:

B: I sense that even though I know that he is an evolved soul, I have felt and have a strong feeling now that we are...Laz, are we soul mates of sorts?

L: Yes. You are getting better at picking up my messaging.

B: [*excited*] Well, here is the question and information that I believe you are giving me in my head. Laz, you told me in the past that I have four soul mates, three that are down here now and one over there. [*long pause*] Are you the one over there?

L: Yes. Much, much better.

B: [*joking*] Do I get an A or what…

L: An E for effort.

B: [*to Shirlet*] That is so cool. [*reluctantly, wanting to go further*] So where are the other three?

L: You chose not to meet them until much later in your life. You wanted to go it alone. Stubborn, I would say.

B: Are they here, and are they close?

L: Yes. There's Jules.

B: Who is Jules? And…[*Shirlet interrupts*]

S: Bud, he's gone.

According to my research, apparently it is not uncommon for a soul who is consistently with us in spirit, or in our own soul grouping, to work and guide us while we are incarnated. In this case, Laz, who is a guide for many, is about to move on in his own soul evolution, so he is working hard with me to ensure that we can stay together. I learned to appreciate that, especially when our discussions became more intense or when he would introduce his soul guide, Ucerous.

In the end it was reassuring to know that this soul not only knew me well but continued to look after me during this life. His protectiveness was a luxury that had been missing for some time, and I welcomed all that I could get. Think about it. If Laz already knows me better than I know myself, does he know what I will ask? Better yet, does he know when I am not completely truthful? As you will see, his style of protectiveness and guidance took many forms and was not always what you or I would expect. "Communication", he would say, "that is our purpose together".

CHAPTER 2

Laz, Why Me?

I found it easy to continue with the meetings and teaching sessions over the years because I was learning something new and often extraordinary every time I visited northern Pennsylvania. However, as I became more familiar with Laz and his guide, U, I could not escape conflicting thoughts about why they had chosen to work with me. Some of the learning was so uncommon, atypical, and thought provoking that I would think someone else should really be cataloguing all of it, not me.

One day Laz and I were talking about the future and what roles I might play as I moved through the remainder of my life. I asked him, "In one word, what is my role in this life cycle?" Without hesitation, he said, "Harmony." Such an interesting word, I thought, but not one I would have chosen. Laz later indicated that I was a healer by choice. He explained that this responsibility would require me to not assume that everyone felt good about their life challenges. Rather, I was to understand when I needed to take a silent pause and just allow the natural progression of healing to take place. I needed to recognize that respecting an individual's soul path and freedom to choose was of equal importance.

Laz and Ucerous referred to the strategic role that soul guides and those incarnated play in this life by telling compelling stories. I joked with Laz about sitting by the campfire and discussing folklore to a group of young children, but he did not return the levity. They both insisted that this task was essential in helping people recover from their experiences and that I would play a part in this practice. I was so doubtful about this future role of storyteller that one evening I focused on just that question.

DIRT, TRUTH, MUSIC AND BUNGEE CORDS

Laz: I'm not crazy just yet, but you may be making me crazy.

Shirlet: There is another guide present. It is Ucerous.

Bud: Oh yeah, U. I have a question for him.

Ucerous: Do what you want.

Whereas Laz has a light approach to most of our discussions, Ucerous is quite serious and always on task. There are very few moments when his guard is down or when he is social. This is represented often in his tone and always by a different look on Shirlet's face. Despite this, I continued to ask him questions to try to understand soul guides.

B: I have a fascination with the purpose of each guide. I was wondering, are you a primary teacher for me, and is Laz studying under you? Exactly what is the connection?

U: Does it matter, and will it complete you?

B: I guess that it doesn't. It is like a puzzle that I am trying to put together in my head to understand what role the two of you play with me.

L: Don't you think you should put yourself together first?

U: You follow me so many times. When will I follow you?

B: [*confused by the turn of events*] Ah…when I have moved more along…

L: Bud, tell me why we brought you here in the beginning.

[*long pause*]

S: He is looking at you, Bud.

B: For many reasons. One, I was lost during that time, and I think there was always a purpose, a button, that was not on my radar screen that needed to be pushed.

L: You were meant to work with us, and you were meant to do something that helps other people. Now you have an idea. Can you perform it?

B: I have some sense of things now that both of you are informing me of things.

L: I am, but you need to make it happen. You know how and who to make it all happen. You can make it solid form. You will not be taking a risk. How is it a risk if you are saving people's lives? If one person gets the message and decides to act with kindness, then you have won. You have a lot of knowledge, and you are smart. People respect you.

B: Some...

U: Here we go...What kind of time do you have? You must get this done tomorrow.

B: [*to Shirlei*] Sometimes he just exhausts me.

S: But he just may be right. I rarely see them team up like this. These two are amazing.

B: [*deflecting and becoming superficial*] Ucerous is here tonight. What does he look like?

S: He has dark hair, and it is wavy. He is wearing a robe, and his feet glow. I don't know why. He looks Greek. Beautiful. He has feet, but they are glowing a pale yellow white.

B: Does the color that a soul project identify a level of soul advancement, and if so, projecting yellow would be what level?

As I have said, Ucerous is relentless, and despite my insistence on avoiding his questioning and hoping for Laz to intervene and rescue me from making permanent commitments, he fires back.

U: I am still waiting for your answer.

S: He is right at it, Bud, and he has no intention to let you distract. He is not budging.

B: I'm thinking…

Ucerous knows that I struggle with the unconventional path he is suggesting and the perception that I might be viewed as odd. I do my best to try and avoid his questioning, but he knows precisely what the real issue is. I am scared.

U: You are thinking that you would like to do this, but you are afraid that your career might be over. You have to make the decision about what the most important thing is. If there is an event that would not allow it to happen, everything would be over anyway, and you would have stopped no one from dying. If you make the decision to do something, you would at least say you could when you did.

B: I don't disagree with that.

U: You know people, and if you started to color this, with our help, it could fly.

B: [*looking for some help*] Laz?

L: If you were able to write about us, it would give us an open road to help. Bud, are you going to do it?

B: Sitting here tonight, I don't see the starting point.

L: You have to think about it. Let's think of it this way. When you go into a job, you analyze the job. You know what needs to be done to make it work, and you make it happen. You are the guy who puts things together and makes it happen. This, Bud, is a piece of cake compared to that.

B: [*reluctantly*] Yes, but this is in an area where I have no experience. I have to learn the immediate frame of reference.

L: You need to call the right people and tell your story. You are the one that can do this. Think of it this way: nothing will come of it unless someone other than another psychic or sage presents the story. If you write it, with your background, it will fly.

The possibility of writing about the spirit world is increasing my anxiety. I am not a professional writer, and there is always the burning question of how others might view me, especially in the professional arena. I know that Shirlet saw a large number of high-powered individuals, and I wondered if over time they might step forward and support my experience.

B: Laz, are there people who Shirlet sees who might validate any writing?

L: Yes.

B: OK, got it.

L and U: When?

L: This is not something that you can sit on. It is important. We did not open you up and have you come for nothing. I have always had faith in you, and you have never let me down.

B: I am curious. Was all this scripted as part of the life that I chose?

L: You finally are getting it.

B: So it has basically been you leading me from Maryland to Virginia and then to Pennsylvania?

L: This was all intent. It was created. That is why I am telling you that if you put your percentages into it, you will not fail.

B: Interesting.

There were other discussions about this writing project, and several more detailed and emotional discussions came later, but the intention was clear. I was meant to find a way to document the experience I was having and share it with others. However, I still have ambivalence about my role. I carry some of that even at this moment. I have a lot of doubt about what was requested, and as time passed my insecurity about sharing it with others grew incrementally.

Some people, including myself, believe that what we are living through this life are iterations of choices that we made prior to coming to this place. This does not remove our free will. Every soul, I am told, selects a primary purpose or area of soul development, and life presents multiple opportunities for the soul to attain those goals. The choices that I make come from my thinking at the time of my life events. Soul guides have taught me that all thought creates solid form, which places the full responsibility for my choices on me alone. Everything I am or have become is a result of what I have created. Boy, if I've heard that once...

CHAPTER 3

My First Spiritual Beatdown

One of the Thai monks told me that to be a true healer I needed to understand tragedy. At that moment, I didn't give it much thought. Maybe I didn't even believe what he was saying. I would learn that tragedy comes in many forms and that some of it is so deeply felt that it shakes you to the core. I am talking about the moment of "internal wake up"—that instant when we systematically begin to see things differently and see ourselves as a mirror image of what we thought we were. Views that we had believed to be permanent turn out to be momentary. What we thought to be desirable no longer seems so, and what we believed to be ourselves is clearly seen to be a matter of featureless elements. As time passed, I hoped I could cross the border of typical truth and into the region of ultimate genuineness where I could see myself for who I truly was. I suspected that continuing this voyage would test me emotionally and spiritually, but I underestimated the amount of self-examination that would be required to find my answers.

The conversation that follows occurred during a period of rapid learning and interesting discussions. My confidence about being able to produce something about myself and sharing it with others was building exponentially. Yes, we were just rolling along, and then this happened. It was a reminder of what the guide Elias taught me that night in Maryland: There are times I just don't see things clearly.

Bud: Laz, can we talk about the writing?

Laz: Yes.

DIRT, TRUTH, MUSIC AND BUNGEE CORDS

I was excited to explain to Laz that I had formulated a plan for the writing project and had actually outlined a fictional story that I was sure would meet the expectation of letting people know about access to their guides. I had given a copy of the writing to a friend with the intention of getting some first impressions.

B: I wrote a lot this month, and I gave part of the material to a friend. The way I try and tell the story is in a novel format, and the first draft was haphazard to say the least. Is that a good observation?

L: [*joking*] Like your thoughts. Continue.

B: As I wrote it, I felt like you were there with me.

L: I am always with you.

B: So are we both scattered in terms of the way we were writing the thoughts?

L: No. What is scattered is... Think of it this way. Say we were building a staircase together, and I went to lunch, and you decided to build it going into the wall instead of to the top of the floor. This is what we are seeing.

B: [*to Shirlei*] Meaning he is injecting the idea, but the way I am putting it on paper is faulty? [*back to Laz*] What the gentleman said after reading was, "I can't tell if you are writing a book or a screenplay. You are writing what you see in your head, but it doesn't transfer to words. You see more in your head than what makes it to paper. I'm not getting the whole picture that you see mentally." Does that make sense, Laz?

L: That is what I have been trying to tell you.

S: He is pointing to his head. It all stops there.

B: Can I tell you both about the writing? It has three characters: Marr, Jules, and Linin.

L: Listening.

S: He is not moving. He is floating.

Feeling anxious about his receptivity, and having already heard about the staircase, I reverted temporarily back to superficiality.

B: Is he just a light tonight?

S: No, he actually has his robe on with a great light around it. He looks very Roman.

I reluctantly returned to the topic.

B: These characters are composites of many people. And the writing is about truth. It is a story, but in the content there is a search for the truth within the world they live in. What is the truth that people really believe? What is the truth about how we understand other people and the way that we are governed? But the only way to get to those answers is to answer your own truth. It is the exploration of these people taking a look at the situation they are in but having to examine themselves.

L: I want to ask you something. Why didn't you write all our names into the story and talk about us and use this as a serious experience? They would have been well received.

B: [*to Shirley*] Laz is in the book, and he is himself.

L: We should have been who we are. It would have been a shame to give us this way. If you had it more on a physical approach and this was what we are doing and this is what is happening now, people would buy it because they want to apply it to their lives. They want to see something that is going on now that people are living.

S: You know he is right.

At this point in the dialogue, I became confused. I thought that I had been on the proper course, one that I felt was comfortable and could possibly get the message across. Plus, I thoroughly enjoyed the creation of a scenario that did not require any personal disclosure. I knew a conflict was coming, and I started to dig in. This was a bad mistake.

B: [*to Shirlet*] I can tell you what I was thinking. In my mind, creating this story, the search for truth, and supposing that this writing is successful and things go public and people say, "How did you come to this story?" I could relate it to what most people don't talk about: our soul guides.

L: You still do not understand my question. Why isn't this just all of you?

S: Remember, he said it is all just thoughts in your head. Why isn't it out in the living? Why isn't it just real life with what is happening now? Why don't you go further? That is what he is talking about.

B: I don't have an answer for that. When I took the form of a story, it just became easier for me.

L: Why?

B: It just was.

L: You're hiding.

B: No, I'm not.

There are times when I get defensive, and this was certainly one of them. I hate making mistakes. When I do, my analytical thinking takes over and develops all kinds of self-protective measures. Although I could see both Laz and Shirlet's points of view, I was becoming more and more determined to make my arguments for the storyline that I was developing. I couldn't be completely wrong...or could I?

L: [*with passion*] You're hiding. It's fear. You should have said, "This is who I am. This is what I have done. This is my experience. This is what I went through. This is who my guides are. This is how the guides want to help people, and this is what has helped us, and this is how it goes." You're hiding.

S: He is speaking very loud.

B: No need to yell, Laz.

L: I would never have done that. People who are here now on this planet want a reality change. They don't want to get lost in a story and lost in a fantasy.

B: I am not understanding why I can't teach about that through a story.

L: Has that worked for you yet?

B: [*reluctantly*] No. When I tell people about this part of my life, they think I'm crazy and misleading.

L: I told you. You are hiding. Who are the people who don't want to work with you? The people who don't want to back you? Why do you care what they think? They are not even 1 percent of the population. You're hiding.

At this point I am beyond defensive, partly because I have possibly offended Laz. Also, not only have I become stubborn in my position, I really do not want to change. When I consider a realistic approach, which will require full disclosure on my part, it frightens me. I know that he might be right, but I push for my position.

B: I'm going to disagree with you. I really believe that if you package all of this in a story that is about a universe, and you build within that story the foundation of what we do here and what you are about and how guides can help you in your life, I think that is a great platform for writing, and people say...

L: [*with patience*] Let me explain it to you so you understand. First of all, I told you it stops in your head. That is why you have these problems. Second of all, they are not even connecting to the story because it should be realistic. Third of all, you are not willing to back something that you truly believe in. That is why you are in your position in life. I am right!

B: If you are saying that I am back-dooring this process, you are right.

L: Got you!

B: I'm back-dooring this. So you are right. What is important is getting the message out. I don't care how I get it out.

L: You are not getting it out. Not only have you put it in the back door, it is in the cellar. Listen to me. We are trying to help you. This is about your life, not just about the story. If you are always taking the back door and hiding, you will never be successful. This is what I have been trying to tell you for five years.

S: Bud, he is really getting into it now. It is unlike Laz.

B: [*to Shirlei*] I know, but why would he let me go forward with the writing for so long?

L: I never told you to write a story. Remember the staircase?

B: But seventy-five thousand words before you say that I have done it wrong.

S: Hold on. It is like a hill you are climbing, and you are about to come to a big stop.

L: This is why I needed you to keep going with it and to hear from someone in the living that it was chaotic and cluttered because you have not changed your life. You are back-dooring your life and hiding in the cellar, like I said, and your back door is cluttered. Any writing that you do is you. Don't you know that is why this is happening?

B: [*defensively*] Yes, and when I review what I have already written, what I see is me.

L: The public doesn't see that. How are you supposed to have your own center if you are running with people under you? If you are not respected for who you are? You can't be a fictitious character and run a healing center.

B: Are you fearful, Laz, that people will not be able to see this as a real thing? That it is all make-believe and full of holes?

L: They will. It is a 100 percent guarantee. They won't have trust in you. You are not understanding all of this. Remember the message from Elias. This is about you. It is not about me or Shirlet or Ucerous. It is about you. They don't know why you are the way you are. Your name is not all over the writing. You have to tell them that you had this experience. You are meant to be an overseer and the rudder to help people. They will not understand it is you. It has got to be you, you, you.

I am so convinced that I should keep writing a fictitious story that I am reaching for any reasonable explanation, never mind a convincing argument. At the same time, I am building my own trap.

B: My response to that is…If I look through that lens, I don't see it as being…I see it as boring.

L: Not so. Are you saying that healing and saving someone's life is boring?

B: No...

L: That being able to communicate with a higher being is boring?

B: That the result of putting it in writing...to try and save someone's life. I don't see the difference between telling a story and trying to tell it through reality.

L: People will look at it and see you for who you are. So when you go where you want to run a business, they are not going to associate you with the writing. That is the problem.

B: From that perspective and that path, you are probably right. [*to Shirlet*] I understand what he is saying, I just don't agree with him.

L: Then write your story like *Star Trek* and all the others that no one follows anymore, and we will see where things go.

B: [*with humor*] *Star Trek* has a convention every year. [*all laughing*]

L: [*sarcastically*] Well then, next time you have an interview, go dressed up like *Star Trek* and go for it.

B: Let's be real here.

I feel backed into a corner and have lost some of my perspective, especially in formulating my questions. Soul guides don't get emotional per se, but they do get definitive and, as always, literal.

L: I have been real from the beginning. I have stated my piece that you are on the wrong path.

S: He has made it very clear.

B: [*joking*] And you like to be right.

L: I have never been wrong about you, thank you very much.

B: The genesis of the writing, as a matter of fact, the starting point you gave me, was "becoming spiritual in the corporate world."

L: Reality corporate world. Do you understand that? Not the Corporate World of Marr.

Marr is a central character in the book that Laz refers to as a fantasy story.

B: You don't have to beat me up. Let's just continue with the discussion.

L: I am.

B: What I tried to create was a world that operated like a corporation...

L: Why don't you just say, "This is my world"? Every corporation I have been with is spiritually flawed.

B: I don't want to be a whiner who is simply disenchanted with the work environment, et cetera.

L: And you are giving me nothing here. I am hanging on the edge.

B: The way to have had a reality writing would have been if you and I had recorded all of these discussions and I simply reported all the learnings.

L: You have.

B: Most of the early ones with the higher beings have been taped over.

L: You remember everything. I can tell you again if you like. You are having problems with credibility. You think they may not take you seriously with a writing about a real situation, and that is why you are hesitant. The problem is you have no credibility now or you would have the life experience you have always wanted, so what is the difference?

B: It's not necessary to beat me up.

L: You can put that in your writing too. That you got a major beat-down and at the end I told you so.

B: If you keep that up, I just may write you out of the story. [*lighthearted*]

L: I would change the writing of it. I have tried to show you. It is not connecting to who you truly are, this fictitious character you've always been, and that's why nothing has worked for you. You are still continuing it.

B: I see it differently. I am not saying I see it right or the right way. I think I can tell my story through that character and have people hear it. I believe that.

L: I didn't say they would not read or hear it. It might be fabulous, but it would give you no credibility in the long run, and you would still be in your position.

S: I don't know what to say, Bud. I can only hear what everybody is saying.

B: He just told me that I spent four months just—

L: No, I didn't. I just said you should have made it reality instead of hiding behind yourself. Now think about it. You are a professional. You are supposed to know all about this. If someone came to you and gave you a false name and gave you a reality that wasn't their own, what would you think of them, while you were looking at that person?

B: From that point…

L: What would your diagnosis be?

B: [*dejected and sarcastic*] Delusional?

L: There you go. I rest my case.

B: If you were trying to hit this straight and hard, then you have been successful.

L: That is what needs to be done here, if you are going to run your own life. You are going to be a healer. You are going to be the go-to guy. How are they going to go to you when they don't know who you are?

B: I never saw that as the objective of all this.

L: Bud, it is the objective. We are here to help you build yourself and your foundation so you can help others. That has been the objective since you started all this.

B: I don't disagree with that piece of the discussion, but there are many paths to that end.

L: But you were taking the wrong road, a very long road, through the mountains and around the woods.

B: You are saying that it was or is the safe road.

L: It is ridiculously safe. There hasn't been a bump in it for twenty years. That is the road you are on.

S: [*laughing*] He can be funny at times.

B: [*concerned and speaking to Shirlet*] Is he angry or just forceful?

S: No, he isn't angry. They don't get that way. He is relaxed, and he is right. Actually you both are right. Do you think you can be successful with that? It's like two different books that the two of you are talking about.

B: I feel like we are two brothers fighting.

S: It's hysterical. No, he is not mad at you. He is just trying to make his point.

L: I will be right. Hmm, let me see. Let me pick up a book at the bookstore.

S: Oh, my goodness! Here we go!

L: Let me pick up a book at the bookstore. I wonder who Marr is. I think I will Google him and find him and ask him for some help. Oh! There isn't anyone like that. Oh! Who is Linin? Who are these people?

B: Let me ask you this, Laz. You go into a bookstore. How many books will you pick up that have some indication of soul guides in them?

L: Up to fifty.

B: I don't think so. A couple of them give a reference to spirit guides, but not many that show some direct communication.

L: Well, then you could be the one who is right.

B: I don't want to be up in the new-age group.

L: Oh! So you want to be in the "this might have happened somewhere, sometime, in your mind" section?

B: I would want to be in the section where everyone reads and have it be—

L: Oh! It's a money thing?

B: No. But the last person to review my writing draft talked about how it read like a screenplay, I could see in my mind how they would portray you.

L: [*joking*] Well, at least that is half of it. That take on it would save it.

B: Short of any reasonable depiction of guide influence, it's a point of avoidance. People would rather—

L: And you are avoiding them. You are right in the front of the line.

B: [*irritated*] That is just not fair. Seriously. That is just not being fair tonight.

L: I'm on point tonight. You just don't like it.

B: No. I don't disagree with you. My preference—

L: You are a sidestepper; just say it.

B: [*to Shirlet*] Laz would like me to put a banner on my car and drive up the interstate…

L: [*playful*] That's a great idea! Think about it. What would you have to lose, and what do you have to gain?

B: [*teasing*] I'd be in the state hospital by the end of the day. [*all laughing*]

L: I don't think so. Why can't you tell people and stick by your true beliefs?

B: Ah…There are some people who know that I have talked with soul guides. There is a larger group who know I have studied with a group of monks. [*to Shirlet*] And these guides, and my monks, are my teachers.

L: You are missing the big point. We are trying to help you teach others, not a fictitious character that doesn't exist.

B: I don't see it as being exclusively a fictitious character. I see it as being me.

L: Then put your name on it like you have on your license in that book.

B: From a byline standpoint, it would be.

L: You are just afraid you will walk into a job and they would say, "This is the nut who wrote the book." Why don't you just tell the truth?

B: If I wrote what I wanted to, I would have no problem. It is about me, but the character is a compromise. It is about me and other people, and it is about real guides that really exist. When they say to me, "I read this part of the book when the guy was standing by the tree and then rolling down the hill and then he went into the water. Where did that come from?" Well, that is something that I did with my guides. Why can't learning come that way?

L: You are still hiding, hiding, hiding. Are you going to take, when you go public, a mask, or are you going to wear a sheet?

B: [*joking*] I am taking a picture of you. A cardboard cutout so you are there with me.

L: You should stick up for yourself more. You're back dragging. The book is amazing. I think it could be incredible. Doing it like a story where nobody gets any type of credit except if someone thinks it was a story is not credible.

S: He doesn't believe that they will believe.

B: I'm getting that message straight on.

S: I can stand up for him, a little bit. I can see what he is saying about possible backlash.

B: I am just trying to be honest with the two or three of you that are here.

S: Ucerous isn't here yet.

B: He would probably beat the crap out of me if he were here. It is an easier story for me to tell, if you want me to be honest. I would have a hard time writing a reality book. I would. I am saying I'm gun-shy. It just flows easier in a story, and I can have all the things we talked about support these people in the book and have that be the teaching/learning about it.

L: I have a compromise.

B: Let me finish my thought, Laz.

L: Let's start over. You write a paragraph in the beginning saying that I am real, who you really are, and who Shirlet is.

B: Like a prologue?

S: Yes. I think he doesn't want to be discounted.

B: I know what he is saying. He knows this. The things that are on public display are not necessarily completely accurate or authentic. [*to Shirlei*] I would need to explain that you see and talk to them. Would you be OK with that?

S: He wants it serious. I do agree with him. I think you need...If I was reading the story for the first time and did not know about this, it would be nice to have a reference in the beginning that this is real.

Although I feel that a compromise would serve the purpose of continuing with a nonrealistic focus on the story and protect me from having to disclose my own reality, I know that in terms of my own development and the soul-guide agenda for me, I need to revisit my approach. I was surprised that Laz negotiated a different slant on the story. Ucerous would never have caved.

B: What does he say about that?

L: Think about it. All thought creates solid form, like I always taught you. You are trying to cease to exist me. If people think I am not really there, I won't be.

S: Oh, I didn't think about that.

B: That is a good point.

S: I think this is very important because I understand from him where he is coming from. You have to watch this stuff, Bud, especially when dealing with an energy like this. It may not be a big deal for you and me, but it is for him.

B: With that in mind, is the message, regardless of approach, truth? Are we at least on the right path with that? People searching for their own truth?

L: Yes.

B: Using soul guides. Using the energy of the soul guide to…

L: Yes.

B: I got the right message. It is how I get the message out there effectively. You want me to be authentic because the story becomes about myself.

S: You really need to tell people how seriously real he is. That needs to be there in a big way. That is the concern. Not how you have written it.

B: It is more about him?

S: They want the people to take it seriously. How amazing he is, how much he has helped you, and that he is the real deal. It makes complete sense. I can see him being odd about that. You understand how people think and what he has taught. We are aware that all this is real, and don't second-guess Laz. Somebody who doesn't know you or doesn't know them will see a book and will read a fairy tale, not something that is happening on this planet. There are others getting the same information that is accurate, so people need to know this.

B: [*stubbornly*] I still think we can tell the story.

L: [*laughing*] Maybe you can tell the story through the beating we are giving you.

S: Hi, Ucerous!

Ucerous: If you ask me, I will give you the answer to all this.

B: Ucerous, we are debating the book.

U: What's the debate?

B: The debate is whether I should write a realistic book about soul guides or whether I can tell a story about guides.

U: That's easy. What have we told you? A story or realism?

B: Well…realism.

U: Then why wouldn't you tell our truths?

B: That has been the discussion.

U: I am asking you that question, not a discussion.

B: Can you tell the truth through a story?

It is a big mistake trying to debate Ucerous. Of all the soul guides I have worked with, he is the most pragmatic and focuses exclusively on teaching and the outcomes of those teachings. He expects action; he is not tolerant, and I sense this mental discussion will not last long.

U: No. I asked you, Why wouldn't you tell what we said and be realistic? Why?

B: It would be more difficult writing for me than telling a story.

U: Why?

B: [*perplexed*] Umm…

U: I didn't know you had cramping in your hands when you told the truth on paper. Why?

B: I don't know whether…I'm going to open myself up here…

S: Laz is laughing.

B: [*to Shirlet*] I know I am about to fumble all over myself because he is so serious and wants a serious answer. [*stuttering*] I think it would be boring.

U: So you are saying I am boring?

B: No. I didn't say that.

U: You just said telling the truth would be boring, and I told you the truth.

B: [*stumbling*] I don't know how to get it out in a manuscript format.

U: How could you not know when you seem to know what I am talking about to you? Has something happened and you developed Alzheimer's?

B: [*trying to lighten the conversation*] That is highly possible.

U: So you are telling me that we are telling you the truth and helping you and you decided not to tell the truth of what we said.

B: [*confused*] No. It is not fear; maybe it is being awkward.

U: Are you lazy?

B: No. For the past several months, I have written—

U: So you are writing truths that are not truths?

B: [*defensively*] I think I am doing a pretty good job of representing it through a story.

U: Why am I a story?

S: [*seeing where everything is going*] Good luck, Bud.

B: Is Laz still here?

S: He is roaring. But Ucerous is not.

B: It started in my mind...

U: We were never in your mind, so we could hear and not hear.

B: [*retreating*] It started with how you become spiritual in a corporate world.

U: And we told you, so why didn't you just tell them what you learned from us as we told you? It is very simple. You need no additional explanation when you are telling the truth. You only need explanation when you fumble it or you are getting around it.

B: I didn't find it—

U: You are telling me my truths you are not finding truthful.

B: No.

U: Then tell me what you are saying then.

B: When I thought about how I would format any writing, in a reality way, it came out like I was whining about how difficult it is in injecting spirituality in a corporate environment.

U: Why not say just that? Do you know that there are companies at this point that are injecting this and that it will be a huge revolution in the future? So you are telling me you are going to hide from something that is coming?

B: No. I could not seem to bridge to the truth. Mentally, I can't always make that bridge.

U: You don't trust your own belief system, and you are afraid that others will not trust you.

B: I think it is fair to say that in the safe confines of this environment, with you, I have a high degree of believability, but when I walk outside and try to explain it to others, it diminishes.

U: You sound like the great prophet Jesus Christ who walked the earth and tried to tell people what they could do, and no one believed him. But I don't remember Jesus Christ walking away from his responsibilities or not sticking to his truths. There have been many other prophets, as well, who have done the same thing, not to mention the millions of martyrs I could mention all night, if we had the time. But you subjecting yourself, by trying to get around something that is vitally important, is very incorrect in the mental capacity of your soul development.

S: He is very clear. He is still looking at you.

B: I know. Laz is sitting back and watching the beatdown.

S: Well, you have to answer him.

B: I don't know how to answer all this. In a word, he is asking me to be courageous.

U: You should not be wearing a lion around your neck; you should be wearing a weasel.

I was hoping that he was using the term weasel as a verb and not to refer to the animal. I could handle "to escape from or evade a situation or obligation." That might apply. But I certainly didn't consider what I was doing to be manipulative or shifty.

B: [*surprised*] That is not fair.

U: I think it is very correct and truthful. Tell me what is not fair about that, and back up what you are about to say.

S: He is livid.

B: [*to Shirlet*] He is telling me that I am taking the coward's way out, and I am not a coward.

U: Then show me that. I haven't seen that yet. I am waiting.

B: [*desperate to get out of this discussion*] I don't want to debate this because I'll lose. [*to Shirlet*] What they are asking me to do is to take a giant step from where I am.

U: Yes, within five years. How many years do you need—fifty, one hundred? I didn't think your clock held that many years on it. Do you want me to build a bridge for you and push you over it?

B: [*making light*] I'm dangling by my fingernails now.

S: Remember, they know years.

B: I'll ask all three of you. Is this what we have been moving toward over the past years? That I am to get the message out of this environment here?

U: I think it started in year one. It has taken you this long to debate it, figure it out, and yet still try and get around it.

B: The truthful answer is I don't…In the writing I use a quote from Kadecious: "No time for doubt."

U: Yet you are the biggest doubter. It is telling the public something that you don't believe because you are doubtful. That's what this is. You just said it.

B: I have doubted that I am the one qualified to deliver the message.

U: If the mailman thought that, no one would get their checks or bills.

B: Why am I the one to deliver this message that way? Why am I choosing to deliver it through the back door?

U: Tell me something that is real. What was the quote you said?

B: "No time for doubt."

U: Then why are you doubting all the time?

B: [*nervous*] It is my biggest fault.

U: You are quoting something that you do not follow. It doesn't matter where you heard it. You quote something that you believe in and follow. Show me you follow it.

B: It is such a hard thing.

S: They are serious. Ucerous doesn't even smile.

B: Because he knows he is right, and he knows how I have been on this.

U: I think you spend too much time thinking about it and talking about it. You are talking yourself out of it and being critical in backing your decisions and what you say.

S: You talk yourself out of it.

B: That is the analytical process I go through.

U: If you want to create something that will be great in writing in the future, and will be worth something that others will value, going through the back door, under the woods, in the stream, or whatever you decided to do, is not the way to the target. What if Jesus Christ said, "Well, I will tell the humans what my father has said, but I will do it and say the guy down the road said it, and he might exist or he might not and if you believe in it good luck, and if you don't you may go to hell, but maybe that doesn't exist either"? Hmm…What would we have gotten out of that message? That's what you are doing.

S: He makes a lot of sense.

B: These are my words, not his. I interpret that as being a coward.

U: I said you should wear the weasel, not the lion.

S: [*to Ucerous*] He wears that to honor Laz so…

U: [*to Shirlet*] Well, good then. He can get his own necklace soon.

B: Why beat me up like this?

U: Why wouldn't I? You have told me a part that you quoted that you do not follow. I am a soul guide and your teacher. I am here to help you and straighten you out so you are in a position where you are needed in the next three years. Hmm…What am I supposed to say? Oh, you are not a weasel, and you did not say that or live that. I don't think that you will get that out of me. My question is why I wouldn't.

B: That goes back to other things you have said to me previously. To not tell me your truth would be a disservice to me.

U: I don't remember ever lying to you. That is not our format. We are not here to waste time. If you are wasting everyone's time by being a coward, then you haven't learned from me.

S: [*becoming more intense*] You can't let all this get to you.

B: I am not going to minimize what he is saying. It is important.

U: You shouldn't. It is huge. Again, I said [*louder*] then you haven't learned anything from me. If you were to follow my teachings, what would you be doing about this?

B: [*to Shirlet*] He is like the teacher who does not give an A. You can always do better and be more. That is U's style, checking whether I am listening.

S: He is looking at you.

U: Answer me. I am listening. You asked me to be here. I don't hear anything but air. Give me something solid. Yes or no. Are you changing?

B: [*nervous*] Ah…I think so…yes. I don't think I can change nearly to the extent that you want me to. I could be changing more.

U: No, you haven't changed to this second. I am asking from this second, will you be the person I have taught? No doubt?

B: [*reluctantly*] I am capable of that.

S: Be careful how you answer him.

U: You are asking me something that is also in the realm of any human consciousness. That is not what I said.

B: [*to Shirlet*] He is asking me, "Can you be the person who removes doubt?"

S: Yes.

B: [*stuttering*] I have never thought about that. Even after it was told to me. I use it a lot with others but not for me.

U: Lives, not truths. They are truths only when you back them.

B: When you actually follow through. I don't know whether I have thought more often about the dynamic of my personal doubt. Once you bring in doubt, you have contaminated your thinking and unleashed a virus.

U: You are right.

B: Just getting it in the front of my mind is a big accomplishment. But like Laz says, that is fine, but you never move it from the frontal lobe and never do anything about it.

S: He said it never leaves your head.

U: So what is your answer to me?

B: To start acting on things without doubt.

U: You did say that. I see the results. I want to see the results. So what is your answer to me?

S: Bud, he wants a definitive answer.

This is an inescapable topic and discussion. I am all over the place with him yet learning at the same time and feeling just terrible. Being definitive is just so hard for me, but he will not relent until I commit to change; I know that.

B: I don't know how to respond to it. I don't want to lie to him. I want to say going forward I have no doubt.

U: But that is what I want to hear. Can you stick to that? Because if you don't, you are a liar and a coward.

B: I wish I had the immediate answer for why it stops in my head before taking action.

U: Answer my question.

B: I don't want to give a lame answer by saying I will try.

U: When you say the word *try*, you have failed. So you say you have hoped you failed. When you say the word *can't*, you have failed. When you say the word *unbelievable*, you don't believe, and you have failed. Hmm, starting to sound like you believe.

B: So it is emphasizing that all thought creates solid form. So you say, "I will not doubt myself anymore."

U: You have to stick with it, not just say it. So now, not understanding the question of the book... What is the question?

S: [*to Bud*] Remember, he wasn't here during all the discussion with Laz.

B: Question is, what is the best platform to get the message out?

U: Tell what we have said. You tell the truth.

S: [*to Ucerous*] He was telling a story. You explain, Bud.

B: Telling through a fictional story but talking about real people.

U: I am real. Why?

B: My best answer is that it came easier to me.

U: It is not about being easier for you. We are not trying to pave the road with chocolate. Do you really think that the easy way out is what you need to pay to put everything across? Was it easy for Jesus Christ to tell the people and take the cross for his convictions? And you're telling me you are not a coward when you are crawling out the back door using everybody in a character mode—that is not correct?

B: [*grudgingly and defensive of the novel*] Yes, that is what I said.

U: I cannot believe that you have the nerve. You have been taught by some of the greatest teachers, one on this planet, me, and other guides who are part of your world and others. Hmm, so you are saying that our word doesn't mean enough to stand up for us, back everybody, and be the forerunner to creating this different illusion and way of thinking?

B: The answer to your question is yes.

U: You cannot tell me that you are not a coward because that is a coward.

B: [*tired of the argument*] I disagree.

U: It is a mental cowardice.

B: Maybe that.

U: You are looking at it in a quick way to tell a story but not be totally involved in it. Back it with your credentials.

B: I was looking at it more from an entertainment standpoint.

U: We are not entertainment!

S: Bud, he just shut down. He's gone. Right out. Oh! He got mad. Sometimes they do that. You have to remember they are very serious, and some people never get to talk to them, so that's a gift for you. Laz left a while ago.

B: U beat the crap out of me. He was relentless.

S: But truthful. I understand because my guides are the same.

B: But sometimes there are no answers.

S: They are right, and that is how it is, and we have to think for ourselves. How can we do the right thing for them? I think that is what comes out of this. You need to be who you are. Authentic.

B: He is saying I need to tell how they exist.

S: Clearly they do not want fictitious characters.

B: You know me. I will try and digest this, and I believe we are back to the beginning of developing writing, maybe using these tapes.

S: Laz was willing to compromise, but U wanted you to do just that. Start from the beginning. He used Jesus Christ as an example. I know that obviously he was way higher than all of us, but U does make it clear. He talked very highly of him; it was really something. I never had a guide talk about him. Jesus backed his convictions and even died for them. Even the great martyrs. Now there is no comparison obviously, but you are being put in a position to represent them. A big path.

B: My doubt becomes, why me?

S: They picked you. You have to remember, Bud, they know every life you have led, and they know you well. Your whole soul, not just this life. So they know your greatest points and all your lives and all your down points. There must be some points that made them want you and know that you are the one.

B: And what? I agreed to do this?

S: Obviously. And they are upset because they think you are fidgeting out of what it is supposed to be within this life, and they don't understand that. It is almost like you and they decided to make something happen with this, and they want follow-through.

B: I always understood that they wanted me to tell a story. I didn't realize exactly what story it was to be.

S: If you are meant to learn from them, then you need to do it correctly.

B: Their issue is credibility.

S: High credibility. Now that he has hammered you on the topic, I can see his point of view. If you create fictitious characters, you will be doing a disservice to him and what he has taught. You are not standing by what you truly believe and backing it.

B: What I wrote, I see now, was very selfish.

S: Remember, it is always about what you have learned from them.

B: Looks like a rewrite. Eh! [*laughing*]

S: You and Laz are like two brothers talking and being jovial. Ucerous is a guide to Laz and a much higher soul, very straightforward, no kidding around. He never said anything that wasn't true. Think about it.

—m—

Challenging might be one word to describe that evening's events, but *humbling* would be more accurate. I'd felt terrible throughout most of the discussion, yet I surprised myself by taking such an active and defensive position on what should be written. Up to that point, I had been reasonably compliant with everything both Laz and U had recommended. Further, I was personally upset with Laz. Why hadn't he indicated to me that I was on the wrong path? After all, it had been his idea to write about all this. Obviously the act of writing anything was less of an issue than accepting the truth of who I was and the accuracy and commitment of my beliefs. Did he want me to see all of my faulty traits so that I would let go of negative attachments? If that was his concern, then I only saw that after the fact. I would review the tapes of that session for months, and it was only then that my emotional hurt subsided and the reality of modifying my position became clear.

Multiple times during my association with these guides, I have had to retreat and remember how to ask questions, not become argumentative, and listen to the real message they were delivering. It is only then that I could choose whether to proceed with what they suggested and understand that the lesson of writing factually about this experience was the portal straight toward the truth about my own life. Laz and U, in their wisdom, had created a parallel representation of my existence, a reality that created a shroud around who I sincerely was and, as a result, who I could be and was entrusted to become. In the end, at that moment I realized how easy it was for me to manufacture a fiction and in so doing avoid the exposure of who I had genuinely turned out to be.

Mirrors abound in the analogies that these guides use, and one quiet night in Southern Chester County, I found myself staring at who I had become. Ironically, Laz was giving me a chance to revise my purpose. Writing about my experience with him was simply a vehicle to get me there. What a gift he had given me.

Surprisingly, this was not nearly as challenging or as contentious as discussions with the early higher guides I had encountered. I just felt more comfortable in debating Laz. You would think, however, that I would have learned from those earlier discussions with "You can call me John" and Hamlin. Nevertheless, the fact that you are reading this in its current format is an indication of how I made up with Ucerous. Courage to admit you are wrong, he would say, is different than bravery; the word courage comes from Latin and means that it resides in your heart, that it is part of you, and to deny that portion of your being can be a painful soul journey, a path you do not want to travel.

CHAPTER 4

Getting a Spiritual Makeover

Recovering from a spiritual beatdown was difficult, but so was absorbing the intention behind such a forceful challenge. It took time for me to recognize the goal of the previous soul guide challenge. After all, my feelings were hurt. I was disturbed and questioning why I had felt an absence of sympathy during the last exchange with Laz and U. The Thai monks had taught me that compassion is not a relationship between a healer and the wounded; it is a relationship between equals. During the discussions surrounding the writing project, I thought—dare I say—that we had become equals. I could not have been more wrong. So why was I feeling that the absence of empathy was being replaced with cruelty? Certainly Laz and Ucerous are not callous. So I searched for the meaning behind the words we had exchanged.

I avoided meeting with Shirlet for some time in an attempt to reorganize any writing projects I was going to undertake and to resolve my distress at Laz's apparent lack of endorsement for what I had accomplished. Eventually, with a sense of trepidation, I returned, but I wanted some answers.

Bud: [*to Shirlet*] I have a question for Laz.

Laz: Not this again.

B: [*to Shirlet*] You learn a lot by interacting with them, but you also—

Shirlet: They can be amazing, but I see only Laz today.

B: My understanding is, as you have taught me, soul guides are always extraordinarily truthful but never to the point of hurting.

S: Yes. Not intentionally.

B: So there is always a sense of compassion wrapped in the message? Or is it more important that they get the full truth out to you so that you can digest it?

L: [*interjecting*] It depends on who I need to be compassionate to, and it depends on what you term as compassion.

B: I see compassion as a kind gesture.

L: I think I am full of them.

B: [*to Shirlet*] I interpret Laz and the others as having a jovial quality to them.

S: He certainly can laugh at some things, and that is rare and nice.

B: It isn't difficult to understand what he says; I just want to make sure that some intention during the jovial qualities wasn't meant to make fun of someone, but meant to get us to understand.

L: Don't you know that the truth always hurts? If you would not give truth, then you would hurt, and then you would not grow either.

B: I find myself thinking about topics that the three of us discuss, that I interpret as harsh, becoming clearer after I have had time to think them over, but at that moment I feel an emotional hurt.

DIRT, TRUTH, MUSIC AND BUNGEE CORDS

Laz wasted little time in getting to the agenda that he had for me. His expectation isn't as simple as "just get over it." His intention is growth and soul accomplishment. That is a hard lesson for me. I expected an emotional response from him to soothe the wounds, but he was right on task, and I was not up for another fight, so I simply moved on.

L: That is because you are scattered. More than once.

B: And I have created the scattering?

L: You are right, and you love it. That is the problem. How can you heal from it if you love to be it?

B: The scattering allows me to not take responsibility?

L: Said rightly. So you are telling me that you have been not responsible your whole life?

S: Unfortunately you walked right into that, Bud, just by the way you formulated the question.

B: The answer to that is yes. I have fewer moments of clarity.

L: The only time you are not cloudy is when you show up with your ego at the job.

B: Well, before we start, let's talk about that. I don't want to find myself living in a box on the street. [*joking*]

L: Not so. Writing will solve some of that, plus you need to plant.

B [*said lightly*] Like a garden?

L: Why not? You plant a seed, and it grows—mentally. I haven't seen you do that.

B: Right now I feel like I am in a fog of sorts.

L: You are regenerating.

S: He is saying you have crashed.

B: What caused the crash?

In the months previous to this meeting, in addition to sorting out my issues with Laz, I had had multiple interventions with family members that took a toll on me emotionally, and I had terminated an employment contract that was not beneficial to either me or my client. Because my eye was off the ball, I was on overload and had an acute sensitivity to change of any kind.

L: Don't you know? Your family member and the last job. You saw it coming, but you were not ready.

B: I thought I handled those issues well.

L: You are just getting used to all of it. You could be a pro by now.

B: If so, Laz, what are some concrete things that I can do to move along on these issues and get more predictable?

L: Look into the mirror.

B: [*pause, and then to Shirlet with a smile*] I knew he was going to say that.

Although it was early in my relationship with Laz, mirrors and self-reflection have become central elements that he emphasizes in arriving at what it true. He wants me to identify exactly what goes wrong in life occurrences that are repetitive.

L: No, look in the mirror, and ask yourself why you keep getting removed from the consultative change-agent jobs, and then ask yourself what trait you keep distributing that is making you have all these losses in your life. Really look at yourself, because without your thinking about changing the events, nothing will change.

B: With both issues I feel a sense of urgency to do and have things more efficient or more predictable.

L: Let me tell you something. Many of the ideas you have are right. But you live in a world that is not ready for your ideas. Sadly, it is stifling for you.

B: So the answer is to dial back what I have been doing?

L: It almost seems like you have to become two people. The person when you walk in who is there to do the job his way, and when you leave, the person you truly are to spiritually develop. But then thus you are not helping anyone grow or saving anyone either. So maybe you have to rethink where you are putting your energy.

B: I have visited that. Am I just not hardwired to be in a helping position or profession?

The guides focus a great deal on how I disperse my energy. Laz has a center of attention that concentrates on the choices that I make and the subsequent ramifications. The role of a change agent in the field of Psychiatry is difficult in and of itself, and if I am making poor choices, then I am in for a rough time.

L: But you are. You have to think a little more. You have to pick one who wants your ideas, who really need you. You have to pick one who wants to grow and change and is serious about it, not one who says it needs change, is glad to have you, and then becomes jealous of you.

B: That seems to be the script. My experience is that most have extreme difficulty changing from their comfort zone.

L: That is true of many. Why are you not the head of the job site?

B: That is not the first time you have asked that.

S: He is serious.

L: I don't understand it. Do you ever think that you are excused, not contract renewed, because you are not meant to be someone's lackey?

B: All three of us know…

L: What is stopping you from showing your result to serious people and getting backers?

B: Fear. The fear of not being able to pull it off.

L: Hmm, for all the time that you have come and asked me what to do, you could have pulled it off by now. How can I give you courage if you lack it?

B: You can't.

L: Then how can you expect to change events? Don't you know the events will change when you have changed in your mind the perception of yourself? See, if you change yourself from the shaking coward in the mirror, you can change the events.

B: [*to Shirlet*] Why is he always coming across as so right, cutting to the heart of the matter with something that I don't want to hear?

L: If I have belief in you, and I know I am a little bit…let's just say "above" those who you deal with…why can't you believe in yourself?

B: I am such a proponent of making sure of what you believe in, yet what you say is true. I can articulate things in a way that people need to be healed, but I can't demonstrate that I believe in myself.

L: Do you know you speak a good speak, you write a good word, and you live up to only a few of them?

B: Hasn't that been a pattern for all my years?

L: Sadly enough, don't you think you are running out of time? How can we get others to not think that?

I want Laz and U to understand that I live with the challenges of how people heal every day with members of my family, but for some reason I am not getting through or Laz wishes to take the discussion in another direction.

B: I have a truthful answer. I continue to work in this field because of my personal experiences including the daily activity I have with my family. I live in that world. It isn't just a job for me; it is something that I live with day to day.

L: So you do, and you are attracted to part of yourself as well, but that is not what I want to talk about. I am talking about your pattern of being separated from the job. What do you think about that?

It is interesting to me that although there are only rare moments when a guide shows anything that I would call emotion, if my personal agenda happens to be emotional, as is the case with a family member, it does not influence the focus they take regarding spiritual development.

B: Again, the story is what it has been. I have been asked to be a change agent in situations where corporate leadership has asked me to do certain things but really did not want to modify their operating process. So the change agent is made vulnerable.

L: Almost sounds like mental illness, doesn't it?

B: Well, it certainly can come across as a justification of the situation.

L: Hmm, if you were the one hiring, and you had to hear all this from someone like you…

B: It would appear as being unrealistic because the change agent doesn't stay very long.

L: [*joking*] See? I knew you would get it.

B: But what is the answer?

L: You just said it.

B: But what is the retort to that? [*jesting*] I don't want to say, "Here I am, and I'm completely unreliable."

S: [*laughing*] I don't think I can take much more of the two of you. Laz is laughing out loud.

B: But if there is an opening for a completely unreliable executive, I am completely qualified. I've been removed from contracts from the last three, and I'm looking for a fourth.

S: He's roaring. I need to take a breath.

L: Well, if you had to tell the truth, maybe that is what you needed to say. I think the biggest thing is why, at your age, are you looking for this kind of work?

B: I want to work. I like what I do, and I'm good at it.

L: Doesn't it make you sad when you look into the mirror and you see that you have accomplished so much but nothing for yourself?

B: In my private moments I reflect on that.

L: Bluntly put, you are at your age, you have no one in your life now, and you are single. But you have a good home, you have a vehicle that thanks to me didn't die along with yourself, and you actually have character and somewhat of a peace of mind to help other living things. But what you lack is anything that is to do with you moving along with your life at an acceptable pace and gaining knowledge, gaining employment, gaining love. You lack it; it is not there. So you are asking me how you can create it, but if you look at your past, you haven't created that ever.

S: He means long-term.

B: I'm not trying to find a smart answer to any of this...

L: So I think the question here is how can we redo Bud completely, mentally, and emotionally for himself?

B: I feel like a makeover.

S: [*surprised*] Oh! Ucerous is here. That is pretty cool that they are here together.

B: Age aside, Laz is saying I haven't been able to do it up to this time. I need a makeover. I need to examine myself so I don't keep making the same mistakes.

U: Tell me what you think a makeover would be.

I always feel some trepidation when Ucerous shows up unannounced. He is a no-nonsense soul guide and teacher who is more advanced than Laz. While he is there, I expect the humor may leave the discussion, and often Laz will take a backseat. What Ucerous has to offer will be serious, and I really wasn't prepared for that level of soul examination during this meeting.

B: Ah! [*stuttering*] Don't laugh...

S: Ucerous isn't, but Laz is.

B: U is probably already in my head and knows what I will be saying.

S: Ucerous is very serious actually.

B: I need to reexamine the way I think about all of this.

U: All you ever do is examine yourself, but you never come to any conclusions to change it. Why?

B: [*pause*] At times I am lazy. My pattern has always been to think it through but not take the next step to implement something.

U: So you are saying your thought patterns are not complete?

B: Absolutely. It doesn't complete at the point of action. At the point of thinking, I will completely overanalyze anything.

U: Don't you know that only you can?

B: I think that is what frustrates me most times, that I know that, and part of me doesn't know why I fail to act other than fear of doing something out of my comfort zone.

U: As far as your age goes, that is not relevant. Human existence is actually quite short compared to what it was meant to be, and I could get into that for days and months and years and you still would not be able to apply it. For your age of spiritual and mental development, you are very much lacking, and you're only lacking because it is like a group of stairs. I notice you getting halfway up them, and you stop, and you come back down, but you never get to the top. That is something ingrained in you, a seed that won't grow, and you have to ask yourself how you can merge to make that happen.

B: Is it as simple as the fear of failure to move forward?

U: It is. Don't you know that you have already gone through everything that you can possibly go through in this life? You have almost been killed. You have a family that does not respect you or give a darn about you most of your life, and you have people who pretend to love you and drop you in a minute's notice. You have lost homes that you really cared for, jobs and people who you truly cared for, and been denied the pleasure of love. To put it in a nutshell, you've gone through everything, so I'm not understanding where your fear lies. You've already been there, done that.

B: Is that by design in terms of learning, or is that simply a result of choices I have made in the course of this life?

U: It was you. It was always you.

B: [*to Shirlet*] Are both still here? I have a question. I feel sometimes that my spirit is frustrated over what I am doing in this life.

I opened myself up with that question. I should have been smarter than that. Ucerous is going to jump all over this and, in doing so, will emphasize two aspects of my life that have special meaning for him: why I haven't been more active in changing how to heal people with emotional challenges and my role in my own cocreation.

U: You couldn't be more right. I think humans label things inaccurately. It is not schizophrenic. Don't you know that the soul is faster than the environment that is cut? Your soul is many souls, not one. Many of the voices that people hear are only themselves to give warnings, and they came as such. People who pretend to be medical and in the field on this planet destroy them and lock them up when they have great knowledge. What a shame. You have made it a point not to succeed in your life. You have made it a point not to succeed in love. You have made it a point not to succeed in your endeavors on what you truly wanted for yourself. Maybe somewhat you have gotten some things, but most not. You have made it a point not to succeed in business. It is what you wanted, and you got it. So what do you want from us?

I would have liked to have claimed temporary insanity at that point. The introduction of responsibility for creation is foreign and an area I choose to sidestep if possible. Where is Laz?

- B: [*looking for additional support*] I don't know where Laz is in all this. The way you are talking here, you present it as though this incarnation has been a failure for me.

- U: No, you didn't hear what I have said. You got everything you wanted. You created it. It was a success. That is what you wanted.

- B: So what has this life learning been? Is it a matter of I have learned to…?

- U: You wanted it. You would have never done it if you didn't want it. You would have learned a lesson years ago. So if you really think about it, don't you think, since most humans are only living short lives, that you should have done something by now? You would have learned a lesson if you were going to learn it by now, and you would have made those changes if you were going to change them by now. So what is different all of a sudden?

- B: Did I want to learn and experience failure? Is that what I am doing here?

- U: Maybe you are. Because maybe the next time you are going to help those with failure, and you needed this life and time for this. Did you ever think on the longer plan?

Interesting thought. U can take a real-life truth and lean on me to understand that there just might be broader learning involved.

B: Not as often as I would like to, but I certainly wonder about those experiences in terms of what I am learning. What I am picking up here is whether things happen because of what may have happened before. I rarely look into the future and say maybe I can take this learning going forward. I always look backward. Maybe I was so successful before in a past life...in the next incarnation I wanted to learn what it was like not to be successful in all those things you mentioned.

U: You have created it. You have everything you need. The intelligence you have far surpasses many. You don't look your age in human terms. You are spiritual. We would have never brought you here if you weren't. You have great knowledge of us, and you are willing to talk and communicate with us and take what we say to heart or try to. So you do have some wonderful things about you. I'm not doubting you. I am just telling you that you got exactly what you wanted. You are smart enough that you could have gotten out of it if you truly wanted to, but you didn't.

B: I felt that I didn't because I chose the easier and simple path.

U: So what do you think you are going to do in the future? Do you truly think, as you have said, that with all the years of your existence that all of a sudden you are going to make a change?

B: It is not impossible but difficult to do. I have an existing comfort zone when I am honest. I have to choose differently.

U: Why?

B: Because it is easier to stay the same.

U: So you are asking us to make sure that you have an easy road to develop yourself?

B: [*to Shirlei*] He is accurate. I come here today and ask, "Hey, Laz and U, where do I need to go for my next contract, my next relationship?" They are being very kind by saying, "Bud, get off your ass, and go make the changes necessary." [*both laughing*]

U: Well put. But I don't think you are ready.

B: And why is that?

U: You just answered your own question. Actually, you are living quite easily now. I don't think you can get it easier.

B: If I didn't want to do anything, Ucerous, I would not even come here.

U: Bud, Bud, Bud. We have been round this for years. We haven't seen anything yet. Humor me?

B: I have on many occasions wondered why I made the easier choices.

L: You are lazy.

B: We said that before, and I don't say that you throw a blanket over the discussion and use that as an excuse.

L: You are mentally lazy. You are emotionally lazy. Sometimes physically, but not always. So maybe you have to think about it. Why are you lazy?

B: Comfort?

U: [*to Shirlei*] This is where he taps us.

S: This is on a roll. They look shocked.

L: We cannot be an enabler to you.

B: I understand. [*to Shirlet*] If they were with my continued plan, I would be leading them along the path I've been on.

L: I've developed much in my many years. I would hate to be brought down by you as an anchor.

B: [*to Shirlet*] From a practical standpoint, what I have been doing for the past ninety days is going through the typical research in a simple fashion.

U: Why are you putting your emotions out there and begging for someone to hire you when you could be the one hiring them? I think you are putting too much into this and in such a wrong direction.

B: When you say that, the first thing I see is a blank slate rather than a path that leads somewhere.

U: Don't you know that maybe you should study the path of an architect? An architect is a builder. Someone who creates and builds things, monuments; they build houses; they build incredible buildings. Why don't you study this as an architect building himself and building your dream job? Why don't you look at it a little differently?

B: Laz said before that I should project the ideal job and put it out there.

U: Let me ask you a question. Tell me about the great pyramids. Tell me about building them. Why are they there?

B: I recently read about this.

S: That is why they are asking. It isn't a test.

B: Maybe…

U: No…say they had a vision, and they all stood around and kept talking about it, no one would even have gotten to enjoy it, would they?

B: Are you saying it is like keeping everything in my head?

U: Exactly.

B: So what you are saying, Ucerous, is, "If you think of that in your head, Bud, you need to start mapping it out like an architect would"?

U: One block at a time. If you actually listen to me, you will be where you want to be by the end of the year. I won't say much more about that, but let's see how far you go.

B: That is helpful. All the other debate is making me feel bad. [*to Shirlet*] When they get to the point where they say, "If you have the courage to be different you may find yourself in a more positive position" Is really talking about courage again?

S: He is…

U: Getting up and dusting yourself off, in the subconscious, that is, and telling it is time to get something done.

B: [*to Shirlet*] Is Laz still here?

S: Yes.

B: Can we talk about the writing?

L: I'm listening.

B: Ah! I had a different perception of the writing in the past two weeks that actually got me into a discipline. Were you helpful, Laz, with that?

L: Yes.

S: He looks happy.

B: [*to Shirlet*] What he did, and I hope he confirms this, I was struggling with the discipline because I do not identify myself as a writer. When he asked me to write something about becoming spiritual in the corporate world, it was just too philosophical. When I could create a story, it started getting my mind more organized.

L: I would love to be in the writing. I want them to know that I look good, especially in the sun. [*laughing*] Give them my right side. [*laughing*]

U: Bud, Bud, Bud. Hmm, you have made a great change in that, and I am very proud of you. Where are the other changes?

B: I am not presenting this as a major victory.

U: Why, because it would show no faith in your talents?

B: I just don't want you to think that there was a substantial life change here. I just wanted to say that every day I sit in a writing space and make some contribution to the writing.

U: Actually you just answered your question.

B: What is important is to contribute to the writing of this experience.

U: Not true. It is important to get it out there so others can read it.

B: I find myself getting some mental input from other guides. Is that true, Laz?

L: I am trying to write a book. [*chuckling*]

U: [*to Laz*] Don't make it too easy on him. He has to take full responsibility.

B: [*clowning*] Laz, I'll give you coauthorship if you make it easier.

U: [*sarcastically*] I'm glad that we answered all your questions, and now you will be just fine.

S: I like the way that they take you all the way around and get you in the end.

B: This is truthfulness. Getting to the real truth of it. I've learned to understand, in reflection, what they are trying to get to. I feel somewhat handicapped when I get to the point, now do something about it.

L: I want you to do something for me. I'm giving you homework.

B: [*grinning*] Great!

L: I want you to go to three different places. The first thing you are going to do is to go out to your yard by your old tree. I want you to put your hands in the air and stand there. I want you to try and stand there for twenty minutes to a half hour and not move, and try to feel what the tree feels when it is not moving. I want you to feel what it is like to be stationary and not move. The second thing I want you to do: I want you to go to the countryside, pull over, and get out of your car and find a hill. I want you to roll down it, literally—not to get hurt where there is brush or rocks. A hill that comes down with grass. I want you to roll down it. I want you to sense how it feels to start rolling along. The third thing I want you to do: I want you to go to a stream of running water. I want you to take off your shoes and socks and go into the water up to your ankles or legs, depending on what you want. I want you to stand there and feel how the water is running fast, and it is going somewhere, and it is accomplishing what it needs to do. I want you to experience this. I want you to feel from the tree that you are now where you need to be. You need to feel this to move and get your mind and your subconscious mind to move. You need to know what you need to do to pull out of it.

B: Laz, you know I will do it.

S: [*serious*] He is making it very clear. Do it.

B: With the three tasks, hopefully I will get the energy to move forward.

L: If you do as I said, and you put everything into it, you will.

B: What is this about, Laz? Is it the drawing of the energy from these experiences?

L: Yes. It creates something in you, and they show you how to feel. When you feel how energy feels around you, know what you are vibrating at. You need to start at the tree as you are now, and then you need to go forward.

B: Any time frame?

L: I would like to see it done on a nice day. I am not telling you to do it in the cold or the rain or when you are sick. Pick your day wisely, but from now till next time that you come here to talk to me I would like it done.

B: OK.

L: I feel when you do the three things that I asked, you will be very grateful and know exactly what to do.

S: Very cool.

U: I have something. I would like you to do something a little different. I would like you to do it within the next three days. I think this is very vital for you to go forward. I want you to fill out three résumés, and I want you to fill them out and be truthful and not tell anyone about your failures. That is not where we are going. I want you to explain how good you are and how many people you have helped. I want you to send it to three of the finest places in the country to see what they say.

B: [*hesitating*] I'll do that. My only hesitation is that the finer places are not where I live. Ucerous, is that another way of saying I need to get more specific about what my accomplishments are? Or is this the start of the makeover?

U: You are going to take three balloons. They all have to be yellow. I want you to take a marker, and I want you to write down what happened at each change-agent job. The last three, and why you are no longer there. You don't have to write on the whole balloon. Put a good paragraph on it with the marker. I want you to blow them up and let them go, because as long as you have this in you, it is difficult to go forward.

B: You have used the balloon analogy before. I would like to think that I don't keep all that inside.

U: Not so.

B: Going back and reflecting?

U: When you send the résumés out, make sure that one place is in your area. This needs to be done. No. Let me tell you why the two are going to be at the finest places in the country. It is energy, Bud. It is energy. If you get one of the finest places in the country to even look at your résumé for five minutes, that energy goes on you. That is total success. You're not seeing it for what it is. Then that goes on the place where you really want to go, and guess what? Positive.

S: They actually are telling you how to pull energy from these amazing places into you and a place you are trying to get to and make it happen.

B: I also get that they are trying to tell me that I am not currently generating any energy.

U: You will never go to those interviews, and you will never talk with them personally, maybe over the phone. You cannot go there; it is not your time. But that will help you get what you want.

S: He is very smart.

U: Do the balloons first. First you need to get rid of the negative energy. Then we bring in the positive energy.

B: I get all kinds of homework tasks from these two. [to *Shirlet*] Why are Laz and U working with me right now? I know they don't especially like when I ask that question.

S: Because you are meant to be successful. They are not trying to hurt you in what they say. I think they are shaping you. It is like taking someone and shaping them because you believe in them. They want you to do something great in this world, and it is taking the two of them to do it.

B: Perhaps.

S: Somebody who can understand you and has been with you and connects to you and someone who has never been with you but has your best interests at heart and the power to help you get there.

B: I teeter between whether they are encouraging me or illustrating their disappointment.

S: They don't do that. Disappointment isn't on their radar. I have never had a guide do that. They don't think like that. Perhaps they are wondering why you are disappointed in yourself.

B: I get a continuing sensation about myself that the spirit in me is disappointed in what I have recently been doing.

U: That can be true because if the spirit in you is disappointed in what you are doing here then that would make you a monster, an enabler, and also make you a prisoner in your body. I don't see that. It boils down to laziness, Bud. That is what it is.

B: Hard to believe that I could be harder on myself than he is.

U: It takes a great man to achieve greatness. So how can you achieve greatness if you are not of that scholarship, and why would you hold yourself back from being a great man? I think that is what you need to ask yourself.

B: There is a lot of wisdom in that. If I am to bring some legitimate healing change into my life and not position myself at a place where I will be removed, I need to change. Unfortunately there are times when you are truthful and seldom retained.

U: Would you rather be the bird than the bug on the ground?

B: Especially if you want to make change.

U: Also you can see all, hear all, and know all. And with that input you can do great things, Bud.

S: They are saying you are aiming too low. You need to aim higher.

B: I would like to think that I am leaving tonight not a complete mess.

U: Why would you think that? If you were to be a complete mess and we didn't think we could help you, we never would have come. I don't think you know how great you truly are. If you lined up twenty people and asked them how often they get to talk to their soul guide, tell me how many of them would know what that is; tell me how many of them would have actually done it even once in their life or could do it as much as you have. Hmm, I think you are doing well, Bud.

B: Isn't that the story of the book?

L: Now you have it.

B: That is the story?

S: Amazing.

U: One more thing. Hold out your hand. In one hand you have a full banana, and it is ripe, ready to eat, and never been touched. It is happy in its position. But on the other hand you have one opened, kind of half eaten, and starting to rot. Who has experienced the better life here?

B: Interesting.

U: Think clearly, Bud.

B: The half-eaten banana has had some life experiences and has probably learned some things along the way. The perfect banana hasn't.

U: You answered it correctly. Believe it or not, you're that banana. The banana that is open and rotting is not afraid to go forward with its life. Yes, it might have gotten half eaten; it may be rotting and dying now, but it will never forget the accomplishments it will have. The other one will rot eventually and never have any accomplishments. Sad.

S: They come up with amazing things.

B: [to *Shirlei*] Why the allegory stories?

S: Easier to see. It is their way of showing the bigger picture.

B: I wonder how many times they told the banana story.

U: I will answer you. You are the only one. If it will help the others, use it. Anything we say can be used, Bud, because we are here to help and save life, not take it.

S: One thing guides have told me about all of us is that guides are always trying to talk to us, and most of the ideas we have that are positive are from them, but they are never given credit because most of us are not advanced spiritually to know that they exist.

B: So we interpret them as our own ideas?

S: Sometimes, yes.

—⚘—

With the introduction of Laz, the beatdown, and the makeover as the starting point of my soul-guide adventure, it's easy to conclude that primary guides can be tough and persistent. They are also loving and extremely truthful. At the start I was told not to get involved unless I wanted to hear the absolute truth, and that is exactly what I got.

There are elevated guides who once told me that I had accomplished everything I had intended in this life. One gave me an evolution score of seven out of ten that day, but he also forewarned that I had a "graduate school" to attend, one that would have "homework" in an attempt to further develop and change if necessary. Some of the tasks given in this curriculum of graduate work were simple, some funny, but when all are aligned with the energy of the guide agenda, inspired change is always forthcoming.

There have been a few instances when I did not immediately agree with a soul guide's assessment of my advancement. The beatdown is a good example of that. Once I back off a difficult position and embrace an alternative thought, immediate change and positive movement always seem to occur. So I continued, this time examining the outcome of the homework and what lesson my soul guides had intended.

CHAPTER 5

A Question of Personal Power

I arrived early one week and shared with Shirlet the results of the task Laz had given me: becoming a tree, rolling down the hill, and standing in the stream. She always smiles with amusement when I report in on my guide homework. For the record, I did exactly what Laz had suggested and was surprised to feel what he obviously had intended.

Standing with my hundred-year-old tree, remaining stationary and facing outward toward the horse farm, I became aware of the strength of the tree and the position I now held within its environment. I was strong and respected but yet immovable, stationary. Because of my position, the view I had of the landscape became limited the longer I stood there. At one point several birds flew over. I was unable to determine whether they went to another tree, to the stream, or to another farm because I could not change position to follow them. There was comfort and power in the position of the tree, but it was for the most part limited.

Rolling down the hill was a childlike event. There is a large mound on my property that has very few obstructions. I admit that I waited a long time to make sure no one was watching and tried to quiet the chuckles that emerged every time I began to lie on the ground.

Determined to complete this portion of the experiment, I rolled down the slope. I noticed, at first, that the ground was firmer than I'd anticipated. There were lumps and small rocks that I could not see while eyeballing the drop in grade, but they certainly could be felt while rolling. I also did not travel the straight path as anticipated. My body is not equally balanced, and because of that I traveled down the slope on an angle. Arriving at the bottom, I felt dizzy from the constant revolving, and it showed in my wobbling legs when I stood upright. Hill rolling is movement, but not always in the direction intended, and it was mixed with the challenges of rocks and lumps if they had not previously been located and navigated properly.

Next I waited for a clear day and traveled to a small stream at a national park. I found a small group of rapids and stood there for a number of minutes to make sure that the park rangers were not around. I sat on the bank for the longest time thinking about what Laz had asked of me. Looking around again, I took off both shoes and socks before I decided to step into the stream. It was hot that day, so as I navigated the bank of the stream and the rocks and as I entered the water there was a refreshing feeling on my shoeless and sockless feet. Closing my eyes, I could sense the movement and power of where the water was going. There seemed to be a unified purpose and direction. I was aware that the movement of the water was not going to be interrupted and no obstacle was going to get in its way. Power and purposeful intention were what I took away from the experience.

Following my energetic discussion with Shirlet, I referred to myself as the rolling hill. The words had just come out of my mouth when I was informed that Laz was there. There are times when what I want to discuss has little to do with what the soul guide has as a teaching agenda. This was one of those times...

Laz: These stations in life that you have done and you have created for yourself are the stations in life that you are in. Verbally, mentally, and emotionally you are the tree at this point. I wanted to show you that you need to roll down the hill to become one with the water. That would really open the path to find who you are in this life.

Bud: I guess what I felt while rolling down the hill was it was the start in the life adventure. I got it as soon as I stood up.

Shirlet: That is what I wanted to tell you. He wanted you to experience it, to know what it was like.

L: With great patience comes great resistance. With great resistance comes great anxiety. So why would any human want both of them?

B: You're talking about patience, resistance, and anxiety all together? [*joking*] That sounds very Buddhist. Is it like having to experience pain to understand joy?

L: I want you to do something for me. Pick up a card from the table. Put the card in your hand, and hold it in the air. Sit back down, and keep it that way. Keep it higher. Now tell me what you are feeling.

B: Ah! Resistance?

L: OK, keep doing it. We will talk while you do that but you have to keep it in the air to hold up your end.

S: He wants to know how long you can keep your arm up there.

B: [*to Shirlet*] He is setting me up for something.

S: Yes, that is exactly what he is doing.

L: Don't you know if you are to be a great teacher with your writings, you need to show others that you have to connect and can do that?

B: When you say "connect," you mean with you?

L: With what I am teaching. You have to become one with all the energy around you. Do you know how many energies are around you?

B: There are times, infrequent, when I am aware of that.

DIRT, TRUTH, MUSIC AND BUNGEE CORDS

I started to relax and concentrate on where Laz was going with this discussion.

S: He is pointing upward, Bud. He wants you to keep your hand up.

L: Now you are getting the point. Now what are you feeling?

B: I am getting a cramp.

L: What position have I put you in?

B: A position of seeing how much I can tolerate?

L: Not so. Look at the situation again.

B: I am uncertain, Laz, help me out.

L: I have put you in a position of a life saver, have I not? Now how have I done that?

B: If I drop the card…

L: You have to stay in that position or you drop the card; therefore, you change the card's life or the card's energy field. But if you don't stay in that position, you could actually hurt the card; yet if you do stay in that position, you could hurt yourself. Hmm, isn't that something that humans are in that position where they have to decide whether they are going to save a life or not?

B: [*to Shirlet*] I wonder whether he is going in a direction that I was thinking while I drove up here.

I was anxious about talking with Laz and U about a family member who had elevated action to the point of requiring possible legal or therapeutic interventions. It had been a source of much thought for most of my meditation prior to coming to visit, and I had intended on discussing it with the guides if the opportunity arose.

L: No. If you drop the ball, who picks it up? If you are the only one there to save that card, and you are in the middle of a field and you drop your hand, and it falls, are you in a position to pick it up? If you are the tree, for instance, who picks it up? Tell me?

B: There is no one to pick it up.

L: Then you need to be in the position to pick it up, don't you? I think that is the answer to your question.

B: That relates to a lot of things. We have talked about my family relationship and those challenges.

L: I wasn't even thinking about that.

B: But I was.

L: I know. This was not for that. This exercise was to show you your greatness. This exercise was to show you that you have the potential to hold things up and be creative and save a life. Do you see that?

B: But don't we all have that capacity?

L: Some have but have given it up. You haven't. You are always on the fence. You can't have that.

B: Explain that to me. I am not sure that I see myself on the fence. [*pause*] How do you see me on the fence?

L: You only do that because of the future work possibilities, and you get really stressed, and you feel like changing your incentive, and you're thinking you are on the wrong path. How do you know that the others are not?

B: All I know is that there are increasingly more moments where I don't believe in the current approach of healing people in the mental health field. Sometimes I feel we have to do some things more radically to help people help themselves.

L: I don't feel that you are meant to work for others. I feel you need to work for you.

B: You have felt that for a while.

S: He is very strong about that. He said what happened to you is consumed in a path of broken bridges.

B: Then I am curious. Have I broken the bridges, or were they not there to begin with?

L: They weren't there to begin with. You need to be the one who repairs them, who holds everything up, like I said. What I am trying to tell you is that you are a foundation for what you are creating on this planet, and you need to align your energy with that foundation. So you need to be all the elements that you are trying to achieve.

B: Laz, are there others like me? Others that align with…say like-minded?

L: Many. Many lost. Many lonely. Many starting the work. Many going forward.

B: [*looking at Shirlet*] Is he going beyond the work environment when he says something like that to me?

Without notice, Laz will change the topic in an attempt to continue with his teaching lesson. Both Laz and U will break my train of thought and circle around to give me the opportunity to examine an issue from many points of view. Perhaps Laz is reading me on a subconscious level because he is always on point. In this instance he refers to the spiritual beatdown session.

L: You thought I hurt you that time, I read. I had to show you that the spirit you have attracted around you, including us, is not going to get or give you anything. The spirit can build the roadblock that opens you to the bridge. You can't even go to the bridge without the spirit. You have to go around it.

B: I'm curious, Laz, how did you think you hurt me that time?

L: By telling you the truth.

B: "That time I was asking you, Laz, in a cryptic way...if sometimes what you say comes across as cruel." But what you said is, "The truth always hurts."

L: Think of it this way. Is it cruel to take any living thing out of its element?

B: Yes, it can be cruel. I believe that any time we use honesty without compassion it can be interpreted as cruel.

L: There you go. So by taking you out of your dimensional and mental element that would be considered thus. But if I didn't take you out of your element and maybe if I left you there, that would have been cruel also, and I would be on the broken bridge.

B: So you are saying that to leave me there would have been worse than telling me the truth the way you did?

L: I am looking at you to build the blocks. I don't see them. What is taking you so long?

B: I don't want to say sidetracked, this is not it, but I have been emotionally absorbed with relationships that have been not going well.

L: There will always be "stuff" going on. Those things are their own doing and their own path. You are there to help and help guide but not to have your path falter.

B: I understand. I am not as good about all this as I should be. I'm not looking for excuses, but sometimes I just emotionally collapse.

L: Humans can't take being rough around people before they collapse. I am trying to make you the foundation. What would the tree say in these situations?

B: The tree would be more narrowly specific, concrete.

L: You are right. You can make it clearer…telling how it is and what needs to be done within the space that has been given and the situation and people in it. OK, what would the hill say?

B: Would have the situation be more adventurous regarding what may need to be done, to break the cycles the people are in but not in a planned manner. It might come across haphazard.

L: Starting out, it might be like a roller coaster, a bumpy ride, and the people should be careful of the end result and what it demands. What would the water say?

B: Much more focused. What is the plan? How do we get there? What do we need to get to where we are going?

L: And let's start it now.

B: Laz, could it ever be a combination of the three?

L: Now let me tell you what I have done in the last few sessions. I just gave you everything you needed to change your life.

S: He is also emphatic that you are still at the tree level, Bud.

L: You haven't done all this yet. I am waiting. When you tell someone to do something within this amount of time, with this type of space, it needs to be honored. If not to honor it is the desired goal, it is an objection to the energy field, if you know what I mean.

B: I also related that back to truth and being truthful. If you say you will do this by this period of time, and you do not hold up your end of the bargain, you are not being truthful to the person, and you are hurting rather than helping. I have done this in my personal life and lost some very special people.

L: The run you have created for yourself in this life is a straight but very crooked angle. Think of it this way. Think of it as you are racing a car against another one, that you are one car and these people are the other, and there is a bump in the road, and the road twists off, one in one direction and one in another. They are happy to go in the other, but you are not, and you try to go through the guardrail and keep on land to see where they are going. It is always a bad position to be in.

B: Yes, it is tough to go through something like that. At what point do you say, "I am going to give up my path in order to try and help or satisfy somebody else"?

L: I think you missed the whole banana. You don't give up your path to help or appease another. Think about it. If there is an earthquake with shaky ground, and you decide to jump in first, how have you helped the people on land?

B: It is an emotional thing I feel sometimes. At what point do I give up my path to try and save a soul? [*to Shirlei*] He is going to say you can never save a soul so...

L: No! I would not say that. [*with emphasis*] That is not what I was going to say. The soul still has to save itself. Obviously you can help and inject yourself in that, and you can save a soul, you can save many, but when do you start to save your own?

B: We have been around this for five years. [*to Shirlet*] His issue is that I don't spend enough time on my own evolution, and he has accused me of this multiple times…

Just as the words rolled out of my mouth, I knew that I was in trouble. Of course he had referred to this many times, but to voluntarily bring it up at this moment was self-imposed suffering on my part, and Laz was going to emphasize the impact of my not listening before.

L: Let me tell you something you won't like. [*waits a moment*] So here we go. You are lonely, you're getting older, and you are running out of excuses to control people and situations, and so you are meant to be highly successful in this life. You're meant to save many people, but you are the boss of that. But for some reason you have decided to become the tree in your home and not connect to doing that and become narrow-minded and see only the paths of others that need help and not yourself, so this will go around the bush for some time till it is mended.

B: I have heard this before, and I am not trying to minimize all this. You are correct.

L: Even everything I have ever asked you, and you know exactly where it was, you felt the right emotions, and you went with it, but I haven't seen you put it in your life. I am still waiting.

B: I know. You watch over me. So just from an observational standpoint, what do you see being the cause for not acting on it?

L: You are easily manipulated into another person's world. Easily distracted.

B: Is that part of my being scattered?

L: Yes.

B: How much of that is fear?

L: Eighty percent out of 100 percent.

B: Overcoming fear is the next step? Can I roll down the hill and take what I've learned as a "lesson" and actually start doing something about it?

L: What was your step after you rolled down the hill and stood up? What did you think?

B: I understood why you made me do it.

L: Then what did you do the next day about it? Nothing.

B: You're right. I took great pleasure in having accomplished all three tasks and that I am smart enough to get the message and then it stopped.

L: Why did it stop there?

B: Fear?

L: How long are you doing the experience?

B: I know. I almost feel paralyzed at times. Sometimes I just don't know what the next step is.

L: Well, I do, but you need to learn it on your own.

B: [*frustrated*] But you are my guide.

L: I have given you lots and lots.

B: [*joking*] Bring your butt down here and…

L: [*playing along*] I have no problem with that. I want to see it for you.

B: Take the tree, et cetera. I take great pleasure in constructive ways to take that experience to others.

L: Bud, you haven't done it for yourself yet. You are trying to teach, but you have not lived it. I am not trying to take away the moment from you because I've watched it, because you need to live it before you can write about it. You need to know your emotions. The thing is you stop after you lived it. It is like you found a ten-dollar bill, were happy for a moment, put it in your pocket, and kept walking. That is not what this is for.

B: But I don't want to take lightly what you are saying. I understand. It is like I see a blank slate in terms of how do I take the next step. Just hearing myself say this sounds silly.

L: Why do you see a blank slate?

B: [*frustrated*] Umm…lazy and fear.

L: So you say you are like the heavy person who sits on the couch with diabetes. When that person moves a little, he or she may get rid of it, he or she may live another ten years, but if not he or she may pass. So if you are in that position emotionally, then maybe you will fail. Is that what you are saying?

B: That's a good analogy, but I don't think that is what I am saying or what I want.

L: That is what I am seeing.

B: But if that is what I wanted, I would not be here.

L: [*teasing*] You would miss me. You need to open yourself up enough so you can hear me.

B: Trying, but my vibration is really off.

L: The place where you live is a good place to capture the vibration. What you have found is a place I would call a sweet spot to raise your vibration and be very diligent and use as a building block to soften your spirit. But for some reason you think, in a sweet spot, you can pull down your energy field. I didn't think that was possible.

B: With me, almost anything is possible. [*giggling*]

L: [*to Shirlet*] This is about a good one. It is about him needing to cut into his own. Instead of coming to everyone else but not to his own. His mind is overaccurate and comes up with great analogies, comes up with great facts. His mind comes up with great words. His mind comes up with great solutions, but they never leave his mind.

B: [*to Shirlet*] He has said this many ways over the years. He says you talk the talk and relate it well to others but not to yourself.

S: We both are a lot like that.

B: I'm not so sure about that...

L: It should not be that way. If you are talking the talk, why aren't you walking the walk? That is what we are trying to get at. You keep telling me "fear," but I see nothing to be afraid of. I've been to your home; there are a couple spirits there, but they have no interest in you. There is no one trying to kill you. Hmm, I don't understand your fear. Can you enlighten me?

B: Looking at work...

L: If you go into it with fear, you will always be immobilized. You have already set yourself up with the building blocks to make it happen. Actually, do you know how your mind works? [*to Shirlet*]

Let me tell him again. The minute you thought something negative, you have set up your failure. I question whether you really want this.

B: No, I actually feel internally odd when I express what I believe when compared to what everyone else is typically doing.

L: Then how come you are not the one running the shops? Let's go back to that.

B: I haven't—

L: The writing will be your opportunity. If you write and get the right message out there, then people will start to say, "Oh, who are you, and what are you teaching?" and you start to disseminate speeches and start to travel. You will have that opportunity to be a leader and the great man you are. You will have to really put your foot forward and get with it.

I have often wondered what advertising agency created the "Be all that you can be" slogan for the US Army. I am convinced that either there was a guide on that planning group or someone who was strongly influenced by one. If I was at a five or a seven on the soul evolutionary scale, from both Laz's and U's points of view, I should be moving quickly toward a six or an eight, if not higher. They would both continue to set my bar higher and higher.

One of my regular challenges in working with Laz and Ucerous has been my difficulty in interpreting their expectations of me. They systematically wanted to see me complete a life task before moving on to their next agenda. I learned that I should not expect accolades from them about what I was trying to accomplish. This was the life that I had chosen. They wanted it completed.

It has become increasingly apparent that Laz and U feel I can accomplish more in my life than I have imagined or feel comfortable with. Even as my life presented delays in accomplishing a soul task, their expectation was always that my soul development outweigh any other plan. Understanding and believing the truth of who I am is the only path to formidable change. It will always be painful for me to experience the faults of life head on because this moves me away from a comfort zone. Hopefully Laz can keep his sense of humor as I negotiate these unfamiliar waters.

CHAPTER 6

Checking In on Elias

As I continued to work with Shirlet, Laz, and U, I also sought to remove any doubt about soul interventions that I had experienced. Honestly, doubt was always part of my assessment of all these discussions. It seemed to be a part of the fabric of who I was and a challenge to try and overcome.

One experience that I wanted resolved, perhaps to test Laz and my area of doubt, was the first experience that early fall morning in Maryland, when I became aware of a window and the guide named Elias. What better way of determining the accuracy of that encounter than to ask Laz and see what he would say? I wanted to know whether he had any knowledge or association with Elias, my introduction guide, and, more importantly, if he was aware of the message he was sending.

> Bud: Laz, there was an occurrence while I was living in Maryland where I thought I saw what looked like a window. I had been stressed and thought perhaps that was the cause. Did that actually happen, or was I just imagining things?
>
> Laz: Yes, I know. Elias had been trying to reach you for some time.
>
> B: [*surprised*] You know his name?
>
> L: Yes.

B: I was unsure about what happened and thought about the message for a very long time.

L: He always shows his message through a vision. Not seeing clearly was important. He tried to connect with you at the house by the water using music and then again with the monk in Virginia, but you didn't listen.

I can remember retreating to the bedroom while living in Maryland, which was very close to the Chester River, and listening to music in an attempt to sort out the fog in my head. It was always a particular CD, and my mind would drift off with a message that I should not be at this place. I had made a terrible mistake by moving to this location but did not know how to escape the set of circumstance in which I found myself. The feeling was similar to what I felt right before I exited Virginia and the Taiwanese monastery, although I sensed it only while meditating with the monks.

B: I also had a mental interpretation of a smooth-skinned Somalian male…

L: I didn't see that. His energy can form anything.

B: I'm also curious…My daughter thought she saw him at an airport. Did that happen?

L: I was not there, but the message was important that she received.

B: Is Elias around? Because I have not…

L: If you need to speak to him, yes. It was important that you listened to him.

B: So he is real, and the moment with the window that I experienced was real?

L: We are all real. When you open up, a vibration changes, and you can connect with different energy, like me.

B: But I am not always interpreting these things, nor are my thoughts aligned...

L: Most are not. It takes concentration, focus, and connection. You are taking baby steps.

This brief dialogue answered several questions that had been burning in my mind for some time, many of them linked to whether I really believed in some of the information I was being exposed to. There were many moments when I tried to test Laz on the accuracy of what was being discussed. That may sound mischievous on my part, but on occasion I would circle around to see if the same answers would be forthcoming. Laz was kind enough to understand what I was doing and continued to work on my overarching issues of doubt. By removing any doubt that I had about the image in Maryland and Elias, I was establishing a true sense of belief in Laz and the information that I was getting.

CHAPTER 7

Symbols

I have been meditating for some years. Sometimes during those silent moments, when the mental chatter seemed to quiet, there would be an instant when I thought Laz or other guides were sending me messages. I couldn't help but wonder if I would ever have a direct line of communication with Laz or U and replicate the relationship that Shirlet had. I brought that to Lazadonton's attention once, and he suggested that I get a small symbol of a lion and keep it with me during my meditation. I remember him telling me, "If you have this lion figure with you, it will act like a direct phone line to me. You will always be able to reach me then."

I have read very little about animal images or totems, and there was only one time when an animal representation was brought up in any of the discussions with guides. Once, while I was working with the guide Hamlin, he said, "I can come to you in the form of a black wolf by your bed while you sleep; then you will understand what I am trying to say." Nervous, Shirlet and I joked about it, but privately I hoped he wasn't serious. Later he indicated that, being a wolf, I would clearly understand. I had passed the animal analogy off as another early learning about how to communicate with the soul guides until the previously mentioned conversation with Laz. Continuing with my journey to solve this guide puzzle, I thought I would probe Laz on the question of animal symbols.

> Bud: [*to Shirlet*] Last time I was here…[*I show her a small medallion of a lion's head*]
>
> Laz: See, I know.

B: I am curious. Why is your symbol a lion?

L: It represents who I am.

B: But what does it mean?

L: You tell me. I'm not leaving. You tell me.

[Pause]

Shirlet: [*smiling*] He is waiting.

B: [*obviously uncertain*] I don't know.

L: [*with a softer voice*] But you do know. Use your mind. You can't give up that easy.

B: [*thinking*] A lion is a leader. It represents strength. It is a majestic African animal.

L: [*softly again*] What does a lion do? Think about it.

B: It takes care of the pride?

L: And?

B: I don't know…

L: I want you to go deep into the lion's mind. You are the lion, and you are in the grass. What are you doing?

B: Surveying.

L: And what would that be called?

B: Observing, watching everything.

L: [*very softly*] I am a watcher. You now know.

B: Way cool!

L: And you said you didn't know.

B: Laz, you and I are close over there. Tell me. Do I have a symbol as well?

L: [*with emphasis*] You do. Tell me what it is.

B: I can say that the only time one was brought to my attention was when Hamlin referred to the wolf. Is it a wolf? Because when he said it, emotionally, I identified with what he was saying.

L: And why?

B: [*all laughing*] Well…It is part of a larger pack. It is a component of one part of the whole. It can work in tandem with others, or it can work alone.

L: More.

B: It is looking for answers, hunting…

L: Now you are getting it. More.

B: And the answers benefit the whole.

L: More.

B: It has a presence such that when identified, other animals take notice.

L: And?

B: It is a respected animal that is seemingly on a purpose, hunting.

L: It is a hunter. It circles, it watches, it hunts, and it pounces. But don't get me wrong, it does not just feed, it feeds the others. You actually identified correctly. You are the hunter, meaning you find what you need to do and accomplish it. You circle it and figure the ups and downs of it to come to a completion that can't be denied, and you pounce. You get the contract, you get the job done, and you feed the others, meaning you share in your work and deeds and your victory.

B: [*to Shirlet*] That is so cool!

L: Symbols are given to us to communicate. Not everybody has the same language, and it is easier to recognize the symbol in a day than to try and learn the language.

B: Why do we have symbols in spirit?

L: It is used in every world, not just yours and ours.

B: If we were presenting to one another as our symbols, we would understand what they represented…

L: It goes further than that. It is mostly energy. Do you know that most beings don't have names, and their name is their energy? As you talk, you can say the components of their energy. Whatever high-pitched scream or sound that they make, it will come because that is their name and how it is pronounced. It all depends on the energy. It is like a spider and its web…how it can feel that there is an intruder coming or its food and it will torque the web, and the spider will know exactly where it is. He is not looking that way but he feels the energy and the vibration. Most energies and most symbols are energy and made of vibration. Everything is a vibration, and with that vibration comes great power. Most beings, their names are either symbols or just a vibration of energy.

That was the only time that we ever talked specifically about my personal animal symbols, and although the sign of the wolf seemed to be a fashionable choice at the time, the explanation that Laz gave seemed to fit most of what I have done. As time passed he would tell me about the adaptability of persona that is necessary for all humans in order to navigate life's difficult or challenging situations. Whereas a wolf might be my desired facade in one set of circumstances, it would not work in all situations. Laz would say, "If you are conflicted over how to understand the environment and the people in it, determine what route you can plot, or what animal you need to be to get the job done. In the end, you will always return to what is your true self if you have acted from the heart."

The most striking part of this conversation about animal symbols was the softness that Laz brought to the topic. It was apparent from Shirlet's tone of voice that this was an important topic for Laz and a very sensitive discussion. He wanted my insight and gently led me to the answers for both the lion and the wolf. Primary guides are lions; they are watchers, looking out for us, protecting us, and making sure we have the opportunity to accomplish our soul path. I can take comfort in that and continue to wear his symbol and hope that he contacts me directly through meditation.

CHAPTER 8

Cocreation through Smudging

The guides and the monks have both emphasized in one form or another that all thought creates solid form and that I create my own reality, despite feelings I may have to the contrary. It would be so much easier if it wasn't only my responsibility. I don't think that I believed in the level of my responsibility until I met Laz. I mean, I understood the words but rarely concentrated on their meaning and certainly never consciously built a plan to ensure that I could get a desired result if I just took full accountability. My failure, Laz would say, was not bringing full attentiveness to my creative forces, and he was accurate. In Virginia he said, "The teachers [Thai monks] conveyed the same about the responsibility of thought and being in the moment; you did not understand that also."

There is an ancient Native American practice where a medicine man, shaman, or village healer would build a fire and meditate to create the sacred process called "smudging." It was a ritual of burning sacred herbs—sweetgrass, sage, or cedar—to produce a cloud of smoke. The shaman would wave a feather in the smoke to carry the prayer to spirit and bring clarity. It was, and is still, a ritual practiced to cleanse the mind, body, and spirit in an effort to enhance sensitivity and, in some instances, alter consciousness. Waving the feather in the smoke helps direct the healer's message and creates the visions necessary for him to fulfill the cleansing.

COCREATION THROUGH SMUDGING

Not surprisingly, there was a point when Laz asked me to light a fire and look for the answer to a pressing question that could not be resolved easily. It was not as extravagant as a Native American ceremony, but nevertheless the outcome surprised both Shirlet and me.

Bud: [*to Shirlet*] Is Laz still here?

Shirlet: Yes.

B: What do you see?

S: Just a light and sandals.

B: Is Ucerous with him?

S: He just said yes.

B: Laz, you asked me to create a fire and get a feather and to stroke the smoke and see what the vision was.

Laz: Yes.

B: Every night I have asked in meditation that the spirit assist in the manifestation and cocreation of that vision, which included a cottage, moving, my daughter, work, and more...

L: So you created it in your thoughts. Once you saw it, you created it. Now the energy you put into it, you will have.

S: Bud, he tricked you into making your own fate. He's smiling.

B: We talked last time about cocreation, which is what you asked of me.

L: Then I've done well. You put a lot into that. Concentrate on your visions; they will happen.

B: [*to Shirlet*] What is odd about this is the more I meditate on it, the less doubt there is.

L: Consider this. If I handed you a balloon, can you make it fly without putting air in it? And I don't mean throwing it.

B: By willing it?

L: Which is?

B: Creating a balloon that can fly in my mind?

L: No! No! Which is?

[*pause*]

L: Energy. So you have an inflated balloon in front of you, which is your vision. You are going to put the energy into it to make it fly and create it. Now it is up to you.

B: Laz, I have another question. When I am meditating on a particular topic, I am trying to project my energy to it. What I feel at those times…I feel heavy. That is the only word to describe it.

L: That is because you are in the atmosphere of your planet, and you are in a human shell. The human shell takes away half of your energy. You have to understand you are not operating on 100 percent frequency, only 50 percent. That is the heaviness you are feeling, your shell and your atmosphere. Your vibrationary level is only thirty, thirty-one, thirty-two frequency. You are trying to inflate your projection of what you want to create and fulfill on a thirty-three, thirty-four frequency. It is very difficult.

B: I shouldn't be discouraged?

L: You should put more into it. Your mind, faith, and trust.

B: I envision a cone, and as it wisps, I am projecting that cone.

L: Now we are getting somewhere.

B: [*to Shirlet*] He said last time that this is a way to communicate more directly.

L: And? You aren't supposed to just stop with what I say. You are supposed to finish my sentence.

B: [*laughing*] You want me to get into your head? You said last time that creating a cone is a way to get a more direct line of communication to the spirit.

L: And? [*pause*] The manifestation of your task.

S: I love when he gives you a run for your money.

L: So you have created a beautiful world for yourself that you are going to create and have. You will not be able to allow someone to take it from you at this point, so you will have to put a lot of energy into it, and you will have to see yourself glowing as a beautiful diamond and visualize people looking at you like you are the one, the best choice, regardless of the position or contract you are seeking. You have to be consistent with this thought pattern.

B: Are there helpful tips to assist me in becoming more consistent in doing this?

L: Yes. I want you to start standing in front of the mirror every night and holding out your hands. I want you to see the other candidates for the jobs. You don't have to know what they look like. Visualize their faces.

S: He is showing me shadows of people.

> L: I want you to visualize that they are looking at you, and you are glowing with a beautiful silvery, glittery light around you, and the others are in the shadows, which makes you stand out.
>
> B: I will give myself an A for effort on this.
>
> L: I will give you an E for effort. Oh! That is what it starts with. [*laughing*] You look better now that you are out of that job. Your energy field is more creative.

I can only guess that Laz felt I was not looking healthy. I can share that he has his moments when he relishes in ribbing me about the fact that my hair is turning gray, but this was the first time that he made reference to my energy field or aura.

[Shirlet pauses]

> B: Is there a problem?
>
> S: He talks Hebrew and Latin sometimes, and it is hard to catch up. Sometimes when they do that, it is hard to remember, and I have to look some things up. I can't always spell it correctly. He is saying the word is "connection."

[Suddenly Ucerous joins the conversation]

> Ucerous: The domination of one's mental frame can create a subjected creation, thereby not allowing you to obtain what is necessary to attune the frequency of your vibration.
>
> B: How can I interpret that? The simplest interpretation is that if you attune your energy to something, you can create it?
>
> U: I said it very simple. I tried to create this question in your mind.
>
> S: That was good. Bud, give yourself credit.

B: [*to Shirlei*] I have a question for Laz. I was reading that guides tend to choose you, and guides are similar to you, a synergy of makeup. Is that accurate?

L: In a way. If I was totally different from you and did not have your interest, how could I help you?

B: Not just interest. We have a similar sense of humor. There are many similarities between the two of us that make it easy.

L: It is. [*kidding*] But I can grow a better flower than you.

B: Laz, last time you asked me to or challenged me to create something. An animal, a bird...Here is what happened. During a run on the bike path, I was saying that I would like to have birds dancing at my feet while I run. The first four or five days, I found or saw birds dancing off the side of the path. Now, it's a park, and there are a lot of birds there. Maybe asking for it to come is a better way of looking at this?

L: Next time you go to the park, I want you to visualize a butterfly coming at you and landing on you. That will show you your ability.

B: Whether it was created or not, it did start to give me confidence regarding the manifestation of the other issues in the smoke, and I think that is your way of getting to that.

L: Yes.

B: Giving me small dosages of belief about creation of things.

L: You can. You will create what and where. While meditating, hold up your hand and bring down the light; there will be seven lights to come down. One for your crown, one for your ethereal frame, one for your ethical frame, one for your chakra...

S: He is talking very fast…Hebrew or Latin.

U: You will connect the energy that you have attuned with. You will connect that energy and the brain to the body you are developed. With that, your systems will connect, making an energy field, an epiphany optimistic…

S: He lost me. He hit me with a word I never heard before. I think what he is saying is to connect with your aura to what is created.

B: A mental process?

U: Your mind runs like a machine, yes?

B: Hard part for me is that my mind tends to be chaotic at times. It is hard to keep focused.

L: Tell me why.

B: I am not disciplined enough.

L: Tell me why. That is why I asked. You should. It is very simple.

B: I don't trust myself? I overanalyze. That seems to be a theme.

L: Listen. You created your mind. If you are the creator of your mind, your brain, and your body…or should I say "cocreator"? Obviously you were created. At this point, wouldn't you know what you have programmed into your own being? If destabilization is what you programmed, you will have to change that, won't you?

B: You are right.

L: So when will you see me?

B: You have said that the only time that will happen is when I can clear my head.

L: Bingo.

S: He is fun. Ucerous, however, is very serious. Extremely.

B: Laz, why did Ucerous come today?

L: He wanted to. Maybe he is grading you. You have a long way to go and a short time to get there. Wait! Isn't that a song? [*laughing*]

Like so many families today, I have a fire pit on the deck behind my house. During the summer and early fall, it is an evening family ritual to end the day by building a small fire and unwinding from work and school. I am tempted during those moments to reflect on the recommendations of Laz and Ucerous. At times I look about for the feather I had used before. The flame of the fire, like the rhythm of water, has a mesmerizing effect on me both physically and spiritually. Ucerous is certain that the state of mind created during moments like these allows for a concrete creation of any set of circumstances. I suspect that the calm creates a particular frequency within us, thereby opening up the potential for thought to create solid form, much like meditation.

One night in Allentown, Pennsylvania, I took a bowl from the kitchen and ventured out to the patio of my apartment. There I placed small pieces of kindling and lit my first smudging fire. I tried to concentrate during my meditation and imagined a moving van, a cottage in the country, a parking lot for work, the selection of staff, a center-city Philadelphia hospital site, and my daughter smiling and happy. Everything came together after that evening, including moving to the farm in Southern Chester County. That experience strongly contributed to the development of a foundation of belief and trust in the smudging practice. Subsequent attempts, however, did not yield the results I had hoped for, and so I stopped doing the practice. Recently Laz reminded me of the success I had and the power that all of us have in the creation of life if we apply our energy. Now when I sit by the fire alone some nights, I remember seeing the certainty of the moving vans, the cottage, and my daughter smiling, and I know that I can create.

CHAPTER 9

Relationships, Bungee Cords, and Married Women

For several weeks prior to a scheduled visit with Shirlet, Pennsylvania had experienced a significant winter storm, and most of the people where I lived were without power for six or more days. When I arrived, I spoke briefly with Shirlet about the strategies that my neighbors had attempted to stay warm. We laughed a lot and talked about all the things necessary to survive the next time. I didn't anticipate that Laz or any other guide would use this experience and tie it to my soul development, but that was a mistake. Laz is always with me and never shy about sharing his opinions. This time he took a midwinter storm and discussed how I prepare for or prevent my life catastrophes. Think about it. How could not having a generator relate to my inability to break away from old relationships through, of all things, a bungee cord?

> Shirlet: [*smiling as Laz appears for her*] Whenever you come Bud, I can't wait to talk with them.
>
> Laz: The reason you have become so uncomfortable with the path you are on is because you have no choice.
>
> Bud: And there is truth in that?

L: Think of it this way. You are writing a script, and you are writing a play. Everything that is happening to you, you wrote. So it is what you wanted.

B: We have discussed this before, Laz, and I guess what I am looking for is the way out. I am not proud of where I am.

L: You don't want out of it. If you wanted out of it, you would not write the play.

B: It is that simple?

L: Don't you know that all of your thoughts create your life, as I have taught you? You create your life every second. Everything that has happened to you this year... [*pause*] Actually, let's refresh. What have you created this last month?

B: I am mentally trying to create a calendar in my mind.

L: That is not what I am asking. I asked what you created that you brought with you and you are happy with. You created every second of your destiny. You created everything that happens to you. You are making it happen. So you tell me, what did you create the last month? If you don't, I'll tell you.

B: [*with hesitation*] Nothing of substance. That is why I came back here. It is like I have stalled out.

L: You created the cold that you experienced during the removal of power. Now let's go over that. Why would that happen? Hmm... You tell me.

B: I didn't do anything preventative. I knew that I needed to do it and was lazy.

L: Correct. So I see that you are not against what I am going to say. You created more laziness.

B: [*to Shirlet*] I know what he is saying [back to Laz] I would not call it laziness, though, Laz. Mentally, I know what some of the things that I need to do. I need to produce it. I have to create other paths. I would use the word *stalled*...

L: *Rut* would be more like it. You are in a mental rut because of everything you have created. So you created your home, and you created the situations. You created yourself almost out of nothing. And I don't mean the true creation of your soul. You know what I mean—your human self that you designed. You created it. Why?

B: Because that is what I wanted?

L: It is, but what happens when you change what you want?

B: Well...things become different when you change what you want.

L: You're right. So if you would have bought a generator, you would have been warm.

B: Laz, is that like when you asked me to create the smoke and wave the feather, everything happened?

S: And you felt comfortable about that.

B: It is almost like I need that level of concentration. I need to have a guidance script. I don't naturally create it. Perhaps it is developing a crutch—

Other guides: Size. You need to size up what exactly you are trying to create.

This comment startled Shirlet. We both did not understand that there was apparently an audience overhearing our conversation. Fortunately it was the only time unidentified souls jumped in, and Laz was quick to clarify the discussion.

L: [*to the other guides*] That is not what he is asking. He is asking for more guidance and confidence. He needs his confidence to be up enough to create what he truly wants—a different path.

L: [*to Bud*] Hmm…that is easier said than done. Let me say why. Look at it this way. Say you had a rock. Hold up the rock in your left hand. Now I want you to look at that rock and tell that rock that you would like it to change into a beautiful flower. Do that now. [*silence*] OK, I am looking down and see that it is still a rock. Why is that?

B: Because I still believe it is a rock? I imagine it as a rock. I don't have the confidence or power to create a flower.

L: That is it. No matter how much guidance I give you, if you don't have confidence in yourself to create the new path, how can we do it?

B: There are two parts to this. I don't have confidence, and the lack of confidence comes from personal issues that are not stable.

L: What you told me then is that you are not ready for creation. You cannot be ready if you do not have true confidence and everything will align with your wish.

B: Is it a control thing for me, Laz? I still feel like I need to control things that have historically gone poorly before I can move on. Moving beyond the history.

L: But you haven't. You haven't at all. You bring it up right now, obviously.

I was befuddled.

RELATIONSHIPS, BUNGEE CORDS, AND MARRIED WOMEN

L: Let me ask you a question. Visualize this. There is a rabbit, and he has the best hole in town. It has plush gardens, and there are flowers, and he loves his hole. He is always in his hole, but there is a better hole in town where everybody hangs out. All the other rabbits come, and there is better food. The rabbit loves his hole. So how am I to convince him to go to the other hole if he thinks his hole is the best when it may not be?

B: The truth is you can't. He has to see that his hole isn't... [*to Shirlet*] He is talking about me, and he wants me to understand that there are other things that I want. That I have to do things differently in order to see the value of the alternatives.

L: That is absolutely correct. But so far, the mental hole you created has kept you in lock and check, like a prison. So when will you break out? That is the question.

B: That is why I am here. I am not pushing it off. When I get in those stalled-out positions, I look for guidance. My vibration is not at a level to change.

L: Hmm...let me contemplate this. You're telling me in so many words...Let me tell you what I am hearing: "I really need a new path. I want real love in my life. I want a good job or higher position, and I want to be happy, but I refuse to budge from the past." So make it happen.

B: [*laughing*] There is some truth in that. [*serious*] Can you give me additional insight to get me out of the rut? I know that to do it is my responsibility.

L: Do I exist?

B: For me? Absolutely.

L: Do I exist on all levels?

B: Yes.

L: Have I told you things that have changed your life?

B: Significantly.

L: Then isn't this the best relationship you can have?

B: Yes.

L: Then with that knowledge alone, don't you think it is enough knowledge to be able to change your drudgery?

B: Yes, and I feel—

L: You are a child with young eyes, Bud, seeking knowledge from a higher being as myself. I understand this; however, as a child with young eyes, you must see the good and the bad. I want you to do something for me. I want you to hold up your hand. I want you to see yourself in the past on your hand, standing and everything you are doing. Look at the past relationship that didn't work out and the heartbreak and the problems and ask yourself, "Why am I still mentally in it?"

B: I have done that. Actually, I did that partly today and over the past several days. I am wondering if that is what is influencing you. Am I revisiting the ugly side of things and reemphasizing that I do not know why I stay in that place?

L: Think of it this way. Think of yourself having a bungee cord attached to your back and the past. You get so far away, and then you get pulled back constantly. That is what is happening.

B: [*to Shirlet*] Either Laz or one of the other guides once told me about a related issue. That if you were standing on the edge of a cliff and a T-Rex was behind you and had not eaten for several days, what would you do? The analogy is clear: Give up and be eaten or take the leap. What Laz is saying is, in order to get to the other side, I need to take the leap.

L: You are afraid of getting hurt. And you are afraid you won't be able to control the next situation because you couldn't control the others. That's your point. Love doesn't need to be controlled. Love is supposed to be spontaneous. Love is supposed to be a gift. It is like the air that you breathe. The feeling of completeness of oneself in a union, and it has nothing to do with control.

B: You once said that I don't show sensitivity.

L: You are like the father with knowledge. Like Father Time. You are not coming off as sexual at all. Yes, you are right. They think of you as an older, knowledgeable man, like a father figure. That will get you nothing.

B: In other words, staying safe?

L: It is the role you want to be in. You want that. You want them to look up to you and say, "Oh! He is so smart. He knows all the answers." But the one that knows the answers doesn't get the girl.

B: But that is also being safe.

L: I think it is more control because you know more than they do, and they have to look up to you, and you like that.

B: Are you saying that I do not make myself vulnerable?

L: Yes!

B: And that goes back to not wanting to be hurt? Is it a shield?

L: Yes. You look at it that way. I think you have created yourself like a Father Time figure when you want to heal and help people, but you are never the one being—

B: Healed or helped.

L: No. You have been healing and helping for years. You might not have known that now. You are never the romancer. You are not romantic. You are not the one women are swooning over. Not the one she can't stop thinking about. Oh! You have made people stop thinking, but not at that level.

B: Was the woman in the other state the only one who ever showed me real romantic love?

L: No. Why would you think that?

B: Because I do not associate that—

L: You have had romantic love in many lifetimes. You had great relationships.

B: I was talking about this lifetime.

L: It was the only one you decided you wanted. That was your decision. Not ours. But then you decided you wanted to be the dictator, the ruler, and the chief. That is what changed the romantic love.

B: So what was the difference between this life and the others?

L: Other lives you were still wise as you are, but you were fun. You were way more fun. You let yourself go. You played with the children. You ran around. You grabbed your wife and swung her around and kissed her and always told her how beautiful she was. You were a very different person. You didn't try to analyze and get into her brain. It is not what you did. You were loving, and you were fun, and you made light of everything. Now you are too serious.

B: There have to be reasons behind that. Did I just not bring that with me, or did I ignore it when I came?

L: No. You have it. You are loads of fun deep, deep, deep down inside.

B: There have been times when I can take myself to that level.

Laz always presented as a male when I inquired. He referred to himself, in our incarnation together, as being a male who loved the company of women. For some reason, he now decided to give his impressions of what women on this planet really appreciate. Perhaps from his perspective, he could see the bigger picture. Regardless, he was going to give me his personal feelings on the matter.

L: Let me tell you something about females of the planet now. Do you know how many males they approach who think they know all? How tired they are of hearing that? How many relationships have they had that have failed drastically and left them lonely or divorced or even widowed with husbands who thought they could run everything? Husbands who wanted to own everything and get what they wanted and never showed any spontaneous development. Never showed any love, cunning, or happiness. That is why they are lonely, and when they meet you, they say, "He is a nice-looking man," and then they start to talk to you, and all of a sudden they are back home again. Hmm...not exactly the person they are looking for.

B: [*to Shirlet*] The irony is he is so right about that. The irony is that, being single, you can watch and sense exactly what he is saying. I don't internalize that I have to be different than that. I look at it analytically and say, "That relationship has worn out its tires."

L: You are totally correct. You need to look at it like you are the guy you are not. When you go on a date, you have to be more fun. You have to laugh. You have to show a vulnerability. You can show your intelligence, but you also have to show vulnerability. If they start to talk about their life, be there for them, but don't dictate it. Tell them exactly what happened, and get off their total tragedies mentally.

B: Many of my female friendships are very much like that. Philosophical. Good word, Laz?

L: There is nothing wrong with that, but when you find the one you want to be with, that can't be part of it.

B: [*to Shirlet*] Is he saying don't lead with that?

L: Not lead with it at all. Do you want to end up with an old, typical librarian? That is what you are attracting. You are not attracting the type of woman you are looking for. What you have to do... Think about this one. Become the woman, mentally, that you are looking for, and then ask yourself, "What are you looking for in a man?" and you will have your perfect answer. Think of her as to how she will look. What she does for a living or type of job. What are her aspirations? What are her dreams, her hopes? Become her for a day, and think of yourself. What kind of person are you looking for? And then you could become that person and actually get someone you could be with forever.

S: That's really cool.

B: If I take my bungee cord and go back, all I see are people who were needy at that period of time. I feel comfortable in that role. You say that creates a desired outcome. What you put out there...

L: [*to Shirlet*] What Bud is putting out there is, "I'm king ruler of the mental frame on earth." No one is dropping what they are doing for that Bud. [*serious*] You change your destiny. You can control that. If you want a beautiful woman who will want to have fun with you and want to be in your life, then be genuine. You have to put that out there.

S: The universe needs to know what you are looking for.

L: When she shows up, you have to show her you have incredible interest and taste, but not just annalistic ones. Don't go all mental.

S: This may be hard for you because it is hard to break out of that pattern.

B: I understand because I have been in touch with what he is saying. I think, for me right now, mental energy goes to stabilizing home.

L: You have strange priorities.

B: I don't know what that means. What I am trying to say is with limited energy to put to things…

L: But then again, you dictated that as well. You created that as well too. Nobody says to you that every day you have to put all your energy into one thing. You decide that.

B: That is control stuff for me?

L: Most of you is still back there. It didn't leave.

Laz took a moment to address one of the primary reasons for my initial visit to Shirlet. I found it interesting that he interlaced many of my primary issues in and out of my soul-path discussions, especially the ones that interfered with my moving on. Here he was referring to a relationship that I had in Maryland just prior to relocating to Pennsylvania and my struggles to come to grips with my accountability for its failure.

B: This is initially why I came here. How do I—?

L: You are not really interested in her. You are more worried about her children and whether they are OK.

B: You might be right.

L: There is nothing wrong with that, Bud. It is just that you have to let go of the line. You are lonely, and you are going back in time when you were not. It is very simple to see. But you are not creating a time when you won't be lonely in the future. This is your downfall.

B: And that is the bungee cord.

L: If everybody lived in the past, Bud, we would have no technology. No cell phones. No television or electricity. Think about it. Somebody has to think out of the box once in a while.

B: [*to Shirlet*] I get encouraged and discouraged at the same time. There is a part of me that just wants Laz to take me by the hand and say, "Look, let me show you exactly what you need to do here."

L: I tell you till you are red, white, and blue like your flag. Unfortunately you will go right back to the past again.

B: But I am here. I don't want to be there.

L: I don't either. You have to have your mind working all the time, trying to pick everything apart. And going back to the other state is a good chance for you to do that. You just continuously pick apart why it didn't work. What it should have been. What is going on now? It is too annalistic. You are actually picking yourself apart.

B: Put that together with the loneliness, and you have a deadly formula. I can go back to all those relationships.

L: I don't understand why you don't have enough confidence in yourself to get someone new and have to date a ghost.

B: Because it is fear. You know that.

L: Mentally, when you are alone, at home, picking them apart, they don't have control over it. Do they?

RELATIONSHIPS, BUNGEE CORDS, AND MARRIED WOMEN

B: [*reluctantly*] No.

L: There you go. Challenging them with any degree of faulty logic only results in a specific task assignment to demonstrate an alternative point of view. Weaving a web of words to try and ward off the real truth stops abruptly and continually returns to the original questions. There is no escaping the truth, nor would they ever allow it. I have a couple of things I want you to do. You want me to hold your hand? I'm going to do that through it and be right there to see you crash and burn or rise to new heights. I want you to go out with someone and not go into your mind.

B: Does it matter—?

L: Oh, Bud! I am ready for any answers you have. I want to see you not go into yourself. Laugh, have fun, and be spontaneous.

B: OK!

S: He's got you.

L: Another thing. I want you to practice, in your mind, that there is a bungee cord attached to you, pulling you back to the past. I want you to visualize that you have a giant pair of scissors, and you are cutting it. Remember that when you cut the cord, it snaps back to them, and don't think about them anymore.

As the meeting wound down, I posed a final question that brought about an interesting dialogue with Laz. It had to do with married women.

B: Laz, why are some men fascinated with married women?

L: Because they are somebody else's problem. Think about it. Look at it this way. Say you are attracted to a married woman, and she is with a man. Say they are having problems, which is what you are attracted to because you are a fixer. They are not getting along. And say they have incredible turmoil. And say, all of a sudden, you look really good to her because you are the one with all the answers. You are someone who can comfort her. You are the one who can help, and you look good. Then as soon as you are married, guess what? You are in the other position, and everybody else looks good to them. Think about it. You want to look better than them. You want to be the person they want to be with. Boy, it goes right to control. The other person is the one who has to take care of them. Always, when engaging with someone new, they must be single. No married women. No women saying they are getting a divorce; otherwise you are just the worm sneaking in the bin.

—⚏—

Putting the past behind me has never been easy for me, especially when the past has a special life meaning. Laz understood that being handicapped and paralyzed by not moving on was the cause for my feeling "stalled out," and this was why he recommended the bungee-cord visualization. Coupled with an overanalytical and controlling mind, I faced a formula for chronic loneliness. I am learning that there are core qualities that I have had for lifetimes that are available to me if my energy is correct. Tapping that resource requires clearing the air of recent perceived deficiencies and paying attention to the counsel of my guides.

Following this conversation, I was convinced that Laz would make a great wingman. He did make one recommendation that placed into context what is necessary to get beyond any historical relationship. He asked me to sit and hold both hands up and imagine that I had a sunflower in each hand. In the right hand was the flower that represented the historical relationship in Maryland. In the left the flower represented my present relationships. At my knees he asked that I imagine sunlight. The sunlight can give its life force to only one flower. "How is that going to happen?" he asked. "How can you make that decision, and what can you do with the other flower that can keep creating life?"

The answer he gave was to ingest all the seeds (the knowledge/memories) from the flower on the right and in doing so absorb everything that needed to be gleaned from that historical connection. "So actually you do not lose any components of that flower; then you can move the sunflower on the left into the light and allow it to flourish." Laz had successfully circled around to an initial question that had drawn me to Shirlet many months ago and had brought me to the concrete reality that I created everything that I experienced, especially in my personal relationships. The safe and subdued rabbit-hole existence I had created lacked anticipation and hovered comfortably in the arena of boredom. My change would require that I find an authentic belief in what could be accomplished if I was to move in a positive direction.

If I believed Laz was real, then I could surely believe in the ability to discard my faults of the past. The Thai monk explained to me that understanding my shadow or the representation of my shadow would be a key to my voyage. His comments fit here. The past is always with me, he advised, but if I continually walk forward in the light, the shadow is forever behind me. As I stand today, everything I have experienced makes me who I am. Going forward, everything that I can be will come from my heart, but just in case that shadow catches me, I have scissors to cut that bungee cord.

CHAPTER 10

On Saving Lives

I grew up a Roman Catholic, learning Latin and even becoming an altar boy. Despite my atypical soul guide journey, Catholic dogma still exists in my belief system. As an example, I asked Laz and U about guardian angels in an attempt to understand the differences between guides and angels. They confirmed that both remain active in trying their best to protect us when their interventions are needed.

I had the misfortune, along with many others, to experience a difficult ice storm for a second year in a row, and, in addition to the road-surface challenges, there were numerous downed trees throughout the county where I reside. Many of us were without power, and the winter advisory from local TV suggested that everyone in the outlining counties of Philadelphia stay at home so that the Philadelphia Electric trucks could get access to downed wires. In spite of the weather conditions and the instructions of authorities, I made the decision to venture out the next day, thinking that I would take advantage of the light traffic.

Unfortunately, after gaining access to the interstate connecting me to major roadways and traveling between sixty and seventy miles per hour, a tree started falling toward my car. In an instant everything seemed to slow down as the tree and all of its limbs came crashing through my front windshield. Glass flew everywhere. It was unavoidable. At the time I remember feeling like the car was in an imaginary bubble as the front portion of the roof partially collapsed. Pulling off to the side of the road, I called the state troopers, AAA, and a very close friend. As they all arrived, universally they asked, "How did you survive without your air bag deploying, and how fast were you going?" Lying in the middle of the road was a three-foot-diameter tree that was the culprit. I know that other people have experienced that "slow motion" feeling during accidents, but there was something different about this experience. It was a sense of certainty. A feeling of protectiveness. So, during my next visit, I was determined to try and find out just what had happened. It was at this session that Laz explained the protective role of guides and the similarity of all guardians.

> Bud: Laz, let me ask you something. That tree and my car, were you involved in that?
>
> Laz: You are not meant to die yet.
>
> B: That is not the question that I asked. Were you involved with that tree and my car?
>
> L: Let's say it was me and two others.
>
> B: I felt that. It was such a weird thing.
>
> L: Doesn't that show you your value? Because if I thought for one minute I was wasting my time with you, I would not have bothered.
>
> B: That tree could have taken my head off.
>
> L: But you are too valuable.
>
> B: I have no understanding of how it didn't take the top of the car off.
>
> L: The car is valuable too. You have given it great energy, and it wants to live. It has a headache on this plane.
>
> B: If I could replay the tape for you, it would be hard to accept what happened. Even the mechanics fixing the car could not understand

how I am still alive. The mechanic said, "I thought the car was parked in a driveway when the tree fell." He was surprised to learn that I was doing seventy on the interstate.

L: Now what is wrong with that picture, by the way?

B: Other than the fact I should not have been out the day after a serious ice storm?

L: And?

B: Doing seventy?

L: Yes. Why would you hate yourself that much to put yourself in that danger? Further, you put the car in danger when it has a living energy. It doesn't want to get hurt or killed either. Why would you put both of you in that position? That is what I am telling you, Bud. Sometimes you do not like yourself. You have to change that.

B: It wasn't intentional.

L: It wasn't unintentional either. Think about it. You created the choice, and you did it. You put yourself and your vehicle in great danger. You are lucky that the vehicle loves you. It will try to recover itself if it can. You were saved by many of us; I'll put it that way. We did it for a great reason. However, you have to get out of your own way. If you are going to do destructive things, there may come a day when we can't intercept you.

B: Be smarter?

L: If you choose to be out in dangerous weather, don't go seventy miles per hour. Cut it in half. If you would have been going slower, the tree would have fallen before you got there, and you would not have been in that position. Let me tell you something. [*getting serious*] If you would have been going two miles per hour faster, you would be dead and over here.

B: I'm not laughing because, at that moment, I knew something intervened.

L: We can only do so much, but we cannot keep you from hurting yourself. I will tell you something. This will not be the last time this happens to you this year. This year will bring wind and storms that will weaken trees and power lines. Remember that I told you that. Remember to check yourself before you go out in weather like that again. Check your destination and how fast to go.

―⁂―

I knew that something had interceded on my behalf when the tree crushed the windshield and roof of my car. I don't recommend anyone duplicate my episode; however, I have had others indicate that during such events there is a certain feeling of protection. I can tell you this: At that time there was a sensation of no doubt. Somehow I knew I was safe.

With all of the cautions Laz gives me, the one that resonates most is that he will not interfere in my decisions or my free will. He will counsel me to avoid trouble areas or behaviors, but the choice of which road to travel is always mine. This theme has been repeated a number of times by both Laz and U. Each soul has a chosen soul path, and despite the concerns of others, including the guides, respect for that soul path is paramount—sort of like the *Star Trek* prime directive of noninterference. Thankfully, Laz and the other guardians saw value in saving my sorry soul so that the path could continue. My take-home learning throughout this brief discussion: Perhaps my instincts need to be considered a category of inspiration from my guides. I can take any action, but always with a high degree of well-thought-out reasonableness, and my thoughts of caution just might be warnings from a watchful Laz.

CHAPTER 11

Communicating with the Inanimate

Laz and the other guides often refer to the power of the energy that is around me and available if I am mindful of its presence. There have been times when they have asked me to try and connect to the energy of trees or certain animals, and, in an effort to learn, I have tried my best to comply. On this night there was a very different request that made me reevaluate the reasons and motives of all energy.

L: Sadly enough, you have to realize your value. I don't think you see it. You see your mental value. Believe it or not, the only value you see is from the neck up. You don't see any other value in your body.

B: Here is something analytical. Why is it, Laz, because you know me better than I know myself, that in this incarnation, I end up with problems when I apparently haven't had the same challenges in other lives. Does it matter?

L: No, it doesn't matter because you are creating your life now. You seem comfortable in it. I think you see and love the power in it and went with it.

B: The power and control?

L: Yes.

B: But don't we learn that somewhere along the way or bring it from another life?

L: That does not mean that you have to follow it. People are many things, but that doesn't mean that they all do it. You can learn from it.

B: Somewhere along the line, either I became very comfortable with it or liked it.

L: No. You like it. You love being the person who can figure it out. You love being the one who can fix something. You love being the one that can get into their head. In your heyday you rolled with it, but you had a lot of loss with it as well.

B: A cost?

L: Big cost. Including your bank account. [*laughing*] I'm just telling you straight out that love is something you will seek. You could very well have it, but you will have to show a different part of you. When is the last time you really communicated with something that usually will not listen?

That was one of those questions that came out of nowhere. It took me several minutes just to try and digest what he was asking. Will not listen? What? So I guessed.

B: Interesting formation of a question. Usually will not listen? The last person I was in a relationship with?

L: No. That is not what I am asking about. I am talking about energy. Do you ever talk to your furniture? Do you know furniture knows everything about you and puts up with you? Do you ever talk to a faucet? How about water? Do you know that the water is alive, like a person, and really breathes and can communicate with you? Do you ever talk to the air you are breathing? Do you ever communicate with something other than someone who is controllable? Do you know that trees communicate constantly with humans and animals? It is just that humans are not open enough to hear or see that.

B: Am I aware of other energies? Suppose for a moment I could turn that on. What happens?

L: In your case? Your mind would think less about going into the past. Because you are surrounded by other energies that may need your help to connect to you.

B: Is there a challenge to get the message from them?

L: Do you know they can get anything to help you or save you and anything to talk to you? Everything around you is made of energy. Every single thing. From a knickknack, a glass, a chair. They are all made of energy. The home you live in is a living body of a vibrating energy field of life. Think about it.

That night was certainly different. I tried to follow his discussion, but it took a long time to digest. It took great contemplation on my part to comprehend all of what he was suggesting. When topics like this get beyond me, I tend to get silly. Certainly, I am not known to hold daily conversations with my kitchen faucet. But I know that the message Laz was conveying was one of respect and acknowledgment that everything is composed of energy.

In that conversation, Laz was trying to elevate my education to show that there is power available if I could only find the way to become less mentally and emotionally cluttered and more receptive. Energy is everything, and I am part of that. There is a common bond that I ignore, and it must be recognized if I am to truly establish my place on this soul path.

I must admit that I wasn't that interested in the hard sciences while in school, so the construction and availability of energy are foreign to me. I would like to think that I am typical in assuming that the material that surrounds me, like the desk I write on, exists because someone has made it. Not for a moment do I assess the components of the desk or the possible existence of energy within it. Throughout his discussions, Laz emphasizes the existence of energy and the importance of my understanding the role that it plays in my life and the lives of those around me. He has a reverence for energy that plays out over my time with him. He claims it is the source, the beginning. It is what everything is created from, and the analogy of the faucet was intended to remind me of this fact. Hidden within his humor are the best of his teachings.

CHAPTER 12

Consultation on Addiction

For a number of years, members of my family of origin and my family of procreation have struggled with addictive substances, and numerous interventions and a trunk full of excuses have brought about only short interludes of respite. Early on I was identified as the resident household expert because of my work and my professional career training; however, mental health and substance abuse education does not protect a cherished family member from addiction or control the choices the person makes. I suspect that I am not alone and that there are times many families face the complex challenges that are brought about by an obsession, whether it's drugs, alcohol, food, or something else. I know that trying to overcome the emotional challenges of dealing with a loved one who is absorbed in an addiction can exhaust every emotion. I needed Laz to give me insight as several family members accelerated into the depths of an overwhelming series of events, and I was not shy about asking. He had helped so many times, and I was convinced he would alter my soul discoveries to give advice on what I could do to relieve the building sentiments at home.

> Bud: [*to Shirlei*] I was hoping that Laz would come this evening and give me some advice on a family situation.

Without hesitation or an explanation of the family situation, Laz jumped right in. What he said was unexpected. As a matter of fact, it flew in the face of many respected psychological theories. I found it interesting that he seemed to be listening to my mind as

CONSULTATION ON ADDICTION

I made the long, tedious drive to northeastern Pennsylvania. Maybe that was his version of watching the game film.

Laz: The only way to heal a family members is to allow them to harm the themselves. You cannot be the dictator and lord over a family members, even though it was meant for good. They do not see it that way, and typically they are controlled by the masses. That is why they seek them.

B: It is like they are addicted to the lifestyle. My involvement is always a safety thing. I know that I cannot control or dictate.

L: I am not talking about the shell. You know that. I am talking about the soul.

B: I think we are saying the same thing.

L: The sad thing about it is that you have enabled these family members. Do you know how?

B: Yes. Financially and by not confronting them.

L: By backing down, you can created a monsters. The sad thing about it is if you had been more aggressive, they would have run anyway.

B: I am sad inside because I did not confront it, and when I did I exploded.

L: You tell me whose fault that is.

B: Mine.

L: Do you know why?

B: I run from confrontations?

L: You let it grow inside. If you would have been talking about it and getting it out all along and making your feelings known, it would have never come to this.

B: I have not learned well here.

L: I don't understand why you run from confrontation when your mental mind could definitely destroy your enemy. [*laughing*] You don't give yourself enough credit. Confrontation does not have to be physical; sometimes mental confrontation is the best of all.

B: My flaw is an innate belief to be liked.

L: Do you think that being liked by someone who has an addiction is truly something that you are looking for? I thought you were a healer, and if you are, then you should not seek that. You should seek to be a helper. Don't you know that all the helpers are not liked on your planet?

B: You're saying I could have done better. I am desperate to learn from this situation so that I don't do it again.

L: Be the trap-door spider.

B: [*surprised*] What? Did you say a trap-door spider?

L: Why not. What's the deal?

Shirlet: He is very good. I think I know where he is going.

I tried to demonstrate with my hands what I thought a trap-door spider does.

L: What they actually do is dig a hole in the ground, and they hide and wait. They are one of the only spiders that do not starve. They are patient, and they always get their prey. Your patience has betrayed you, and now you have none. Being patient and sitting back and inviting them to do their own thing would have made them run to you, listen, and be willing to learn. When you bestow your authorities upon them, it only makes them go farther.

B: Let me ask, Laz. If I could learn to be more patient and less impulsive…

L: You would see your light change. It would open the door for love. And open your door for spiritual connection with me.

B: So the work I have to do with patience also affects my relationships?

L: Absolutely.

B: Why is that, Laz?

L: When you are impatient, you raise your frequency and lower it. It is like a yo-yo. How can I come through the frequency levels to communicate when things are bouncing?

B: Is that why I haven't been able to connect in meditation?

L: Yes. You are disturbed, and Shirlet was disturbed before, and I actually had to guard her house.

In her previous session, drug-related individuals had been hanging around on the street outside Shirlet's residence. It was so disturbing that Shirlet was effectively "off her game" and considerably distracted. We had discussed at that time whether guides ever intervened in situations like that.

L: Sadly, when people come around you who have a lower-vibrational level, they have already attracted dangerous vibration levels in their shell. They are the ones you have to look out for.

B: Laz, can we lose family members to other spirits?

L: I think that they can isolate themselves, but in their minds the family has isolated them. In their mind, we don't want them to have anything. We are the helpers. We are their guides.

B: That seems to be a contradiction.

L: No. If we are the ones trying to help them, and we are keeping them in the house, and we are keeping them away from the bad guys, who are they going to blame? The guys they want to be with or us?

B: So it was inevitable to drift toward those you refer to as bad guys. To prove something to themselves?

L: Actually to prove something to their family. That they do not have control.

B: The answer is the trap-door spider?

L: If they go out into the world and run, and they run into a fence, and the parents are not home, how can they help them? They could not. But if they get them from the fence and bring them back and heal their wounds, then families would have succeeded. Think of it in those terms. Remember that everyone is here for their own soul search, and you cannot keep them from that, regardless of your intentions. You can be there for people, tell them what you think will hurt and offer a door, but you cannot make them take it. If you try to strong-arm or control, that will not work. Humans need to be fulfilled so that they do not require others to satisfy where they are at the present moment.

B: When these people leave us, why is the final emotional response relief?

L: Because of what is following them. Think of it—all the families go through in these situations. They are spiritually growing, and they think they can abuse themselves with substances. They can be with people like that and have so much going on around them. They hurt the homes and hurt all the spirits in the home, some that can't wait for them to leave because of the energy they bring. Families feel what the spirits feel. They are happy that they leave. The person, in this case, felt that the good positive spirits are negative.

B: The pyramid is upside down.

L: If you take away from the soul search, you will be judged on that. That is not the fault of the family. The fault is how the family allows it to affect them.

B: Are there times when emotion is just drained out?

L: They get tired. They need to love themselves. They start to go down the spiritual ladder and judge themselves so much.

—ɷ—

Laz has always been sensitive to the personal issues of my family, but in that short exchange, he turned his focus to the spirit of those involved. Over the years we have talked about many family strategies, which eased my stress. His teaching, however, is always about my spirit growth or spirit path. That isn't to say that we should not do what we can for anyone facing these life challenges. I have learned from him that soul growth and personal truth are found when I have the ability to separate myself from the emotions of a situation. I continue to try to respect individuals' soul paths, but when danger presents itself, I do what most of us would: I take action.

In a later session, Laz would indicate that some individuals had been dealing with these issues for multiple lifetimes and that it was important for their soul learning to find a way to overcome these trials. Any undue or unwarranted interjection on another's part might prohibit the struggling soul's advancement. As painful as it can be for anyone to watch the dismantling of a soul purpose, my family continues to show our love, stand with our family members, and encourage a healthy plan for physical and spiritual healing.

CHAPTER 13

The Asylum

Have you ever wondered why we choose a particular profession? I would like to believe that I went through a conscious selection process based on well-thought-out variables. Sometimes people choose a profession because it is the work of the family, the work that one's father or mother performed. Some choices are probably based on the interests we develop from a young age. As for me, I have always felt that I just fell into it.

Laz and U have suggested that there are times when we carry over a profession from a past life, trying to complete a soul learning. Sometimes, they say, we are expanding on what we have already learned or are teaching others. Regardless of the intention, the focus is on learning. It might not be the identical occupation that we previously held, but it fits into the specific discovery purpose of that current incarnation.

When I inquired about my career choice in the mental health field, Laz mentioned that he had been with me when I worked at what he called an asylum. He referred to it as "the Whitehall." I wanted to pursue this topic, hoping that it might answer some pressing questions about my observations and the feelings I have toward the healing profession of psychiatry.

Bud: Laz, were you with me at the institution?

Laz: No. I didn't go near it. I stayed outside it.

B: I'm talking about the Whitehall Institution or Asylum.

L: I would not go in.

B: I am curious. Why would I choose to go and work there during that lifetime?

L: Because you are stubborn. [*smiling*]

B: Did I think I could do some things that others could not?

L: You did. You always have.

B: Is that a trait that I carry forward into other incarnations?

L: Yes.

Earlier in the discussion, Laz and I had been talking about my inability to consistently connect with him, which led to him bring up his symbol, the lion.

L: My symbol is a lion. If you have a symbol with a lion on it and always wear it, you will always be able to call on me through it, and together we can talk more about this.

B: Why did it take so long to start this part of my—?

L: Fear. You always had it in you, but you didn't want to step on anyone's toes or rock the boat. You didn't trust your own mind. You have to remember that you have worked with a lot of insanity-type situations, so you wondered about your own.

B: In this shell?

L: Yes. Plus, during that time at Whitehall, you were appalled at the conditions. People would be without clothing; they would be lying in their body fluids. The caretakers were not careful. You chose to stay with this throughout this life to try and make a difference.

B: To try and make things better now?

L: Why do you think you find yourself in what you call a change-agent role? Stubborn, I say.

B: But changing the healing is so...

L: Difficult? Think about it. Who really wants to change? That is why you move on.

B: I'm thinking, Laz, but cannot remember a facility called Whitehall. Where would this have been?

L: Are you thinking that Whitehall is something materialistic that exists on your planet? Not only were they treated poorly, they should not have been there to begin with. This I quote to you: "I go back very far. I am ancient. I am light. I am around you. I am substance. I am earth." I can tell you some of what was going on, and I shall do this.

Shirlet: I don't know where that came from, Bud.

B: [*determined to get an answer*] But was there a place called Whitehall?

L: That was not the true name of what it was. The name was given to that as such for the nurse. She was our light. She helped people. She gave life. She corrected things. She made people better. Many people died there and should have lived. It was such a bad position. It was a stifling part of humanity to have put them there. This was a subject that was a bad matter and almost destroyed you mentally, emotionally, and physically. The position that you were in drove you to a different part of yourself that you were not proud of.

B: Was I an active participant in the mistreatment or allowing mistreatment to continue?

L: You were an active participant in being there and going with the flow of something you were incredibly against.

B: Was I one of the treating physicians?

L: Sadly enough. It was called Whitehall. It was what you now call a state hospital.

B: Which one?

L: Jersey. The treatment of the people was of such to a vagrant with no home. Children crawled on the floor who should not have been there. It was a tragedy on humanity.

B: Laz, could this be Greystone?

L: A sad place. Some were used as guinea pigs. You should go there sometime and ask to just walk through it. I will be with you and protect you.

B: Perhaps.

L: Bud, you are a changer; do not waste your time with avenues that do not want to change unless you are willing to be an actor and just go for the money.

—∞—

Over the years, I have served as CEO for a number of psychiatric hospitals and have operated numerous mental health clinics. My focus has always been on doing things better by using an integrated transformational process on an individual facility basis. When Laz mentioned the asylum, my eyes opened, and suddenly my career choice seemed to make more sense. Choosing to be a change agent, however, is not easy, especially when much of the mental health industry is comfortable exactly as it is. Both Laz and

U have addressed the human healing process on multiple occasions, and in a later chapter I reveal how they dealt with it head on and in more detail.

When I listen to this tape, which I do on occasion, I become contemplative about the career path I am on. It may be by direct intention that I gravitated to mental health operations that needed to address the means by which they attempted to treat and heal. My daughter is fond of saying that I always work where things are broken. Maybe that is by design as well. Maybe my soul journey is to make a personal difference this time and draw attention to the mistreatments and inappropriate polypharmacy interventions that take place.

I find that I have a low tolerance when mental health treatment is not individualized to the person and simply becomes "the way we do things here." No soul life or soul advancement should be interrupted because of ignorance within the layers of our medical industry. We are better than that, and although we have grown light years from the story of Whitehall or Greystone, there is still much more to do. Whether I visit this hospital is still open for discussion. Changing the dialogue and approach we have toward emotional healing is a worthwhile use of my energy, but it is reassuring to know that Laz would travel with me.

CHAPTER 14

Where Do Guides Rest?

From what I have learned, being a soul guide is a full-time and all-consuming job. Laz has said that he is a guide to many and that I cannot comprehend that all time is happening now, but if I could, his "job" would make more sense.

I tried to gather as much information about his existence as possible, hoping to learn more about my former brother. With my immature and obsessive curiosity, I was determined to understand what he does when he's not looking after me. After all, I just might be joining him someday.

Occasionally Laz and U will allow the conversation to diverge from its focus on me. During that time some of my questions seem to slip by them, and their answers have given me a glimpse into their world. This was one instance.

> Bud: Laz, this is an odd question, but where do you go when you want to rest?
>
> Laz: [*surprised*] Where do I go?
>
> B: Yes.
>
> L: I can't leave as long as you are here, and the others. But when you are all with me, I can rest on my dimensional level. It is a beautiful city. It is just like this one, only no crime or problems, and everything is living. It is living energy. It is not what you see. The

colors are the most beautiful that you have ever seen. The jewels are everywhere. The people use them to heal. It is not about greed or selling. Crystal actually helps you. It restores your energy. Everything is used in a positive way.

[pause]

L: I love the crystal city. That is the most beautiful. Think of a city made of crystal. The most beautiful crystals you have ever seen. The architecture, the streets, they glow, and they are alive. It is breathtaking.

B: Is that something that we all create when we are there?

L: I think the higher ones create this.

B: I have always thought that what we see is what we feel comfortable or familiar with.

L: What you see when you pass is where you get put. It is not about comfortable. What you see in the living sense is what you create when passed.

B: Laz, when you and I and the other two in our group are together, are there places that we go together?

L: Yes.

B: Are there planets? Dimensions?

L: Yes and yes.

B: Is there a favorite place to go?

L: It depends on your development and where they allow you to be. There is a group of thirteen, the council, and they make that decision, not us. You are judged by your works, and you are put accordingly, that is true.

—∞—

I can't say I like the idea of having a soul committee determining when and where I can travel; however, I previously read about a guiding council that we interact with both before we incarnate and when we return to our spiritual home. I presume that I will have the ability to hang out with Laz "over there" and that I just need to inquire more about the process of how we get to move about. Maybe I've found my first question for the council upon my return.

The complexity of the dimensions that Laz occupies fascinates me and energizes my inquisitiveness. As much as my thoughts gravitate toward understanding his spacious existence, perhaps it would be more productive to inquire as to why I maintain such an odd wonderment about his world. Laz often indicated to me that if my snooping had the capacity to make me whole, the prying was worth the effort. I'm not so sure that in this instance it wasn't just pure superficiality and a tad bit of avoidance. After all, redirecting the attention to Laz takes the light off me. Yeah, right...

CHAPTER 15

Remembering Maurin Pesta

There are times when my mind wanders and summons up events and people from my past. One highly emotional recollection involved a young girl from my childhood neighborhood. We were the same age and attended the same high school. While she was very attractive, we never dated throughout our teen years. I was a punk kid growing up on the street corners of a deteriorating steel town, and she was much more responsible, and because of that we socialized in different groups.

Many years later, as I sit on the front porch of my farm and face the apple trees, I think of Maurin Pesta. It isn't an obsession. It is an internal sensation…a connection that comes through that growing fruit tree yet has no long-standing life attachment. What is it about those thoughts that seem to be the pestering splinters that pinch my mind? Where do they come from?

In her early twenties, Maurin was diagnosed with a terminal case of cancer. I don't remember the type; I just remember that she had to make a very difficult decision regarding treatment. Having returned from college in Iowa, I took her to the movies and out to eat at the request of others. Don't get the wrong impression—I wasn't doing her a favor; she was doing one for me. I remember that while I was with Maurin, I felt extremely emotional and awkward about her condition. I was not familiar with terminal illnesses and didn't know how to bridge my feeling with what she was surely feeling. She died in June 1972, and, along with many others, I was very sad.

With a continual mental image of this very sensitive and beautiful girl in my mind, I tried to come to grips with why she occupied my time by the tree. After all, multiple decades had passed since she died. Surely Laz would have a reasonable answer regarding this mental shard. So when the time was right, I took the opportunity to ask him why these thoughts seemed to persist when so many relationships and so much time had passed. Why Maurin? And what was it about that apple tree?

> Bud: Laz, there has been a woman constantly in my mind that I have been remembering lately. She died young. Her name was Maurin Pesta.
>
> Shirlet: Such a beautiful name.
>
> B: She passed in her early twenties. Why does she always come up in my head and especially while I am meditating by the apple tree? It is almost like she is there with me or part of the tree.
>
> Laz: Because you wanted her. And you wanted her to be there.
>
> B: What? [*pause*] I'm not sure about the wanting part.
>
> L: You did. You two have a connection, but it is not a soul-mate connection and not so strong in this incarnation. You really liked her, multiple times. Your subconscious mind connected to her and the healing you wanted to do to help her. That had a lot to do with it.
>
> B: Are you saying I had a past life with her?
>
> L: Yes. You were in many loving relationships together; that is why you felt really bad for her in this life. And conflicted. You loved her very much in other lives.
>
> B: I felt paralyzed because she was dying, and there was nothing to do. I had the same feeling everyone else did about her disease, but I wanted to be with her. Laz, is Maurin still there with you in spirit?

L: Yes. She is so grateful to you. She thinks a lot about you and cares deeply for you.

B: I still feel her. It is a comfort, when I meditate.

L: You made her happy for that period of time, Bud. She is saying, "Thank you."

B: She is so very welcome. This is so excellent.

Maurin Pesta. Someone who passed through my life at a time when I was ill equipped to bring the kind of comfort she really required or deserved. Yet when I find the need for private comfort, her energy is present. As Laz suggested, she might not be a mate who is part of my soul grouping, but she illustrates the depth of the connection that all souls have as we pass through our lives.

I now reserve separate meditation time just for Maurin, and I feel the love that was shared and maintained over all those lives. In the movie *Ghost*, Patrick Swayze's character, Sam Wheat, says to Molly, played by Demi Moore, "Molly, it's amazing, the love inside; you take it with you." That is the gift Maurin gives me every time I meditate by the apple tree—the love of many past lifetimes shared by two souls who, for whatever reason, continue to connect and express their affection for each other. I guess you could say that Maurin still lives with me at those moments by the tree. It's such a special feeling to know that she is there.

If we believe that we have souls, and I do, then surely they are made up of love. If that is true, then a large part of my spirit is comprised of the tenderness I once shared with Maurin.

CHAPTER 16

A Peek at the Future

I have said previously that soul guides do not have an interest in predicting any specific future events. They are not psychics. That is not their role. They indicated that the reason for taking such a position is our free will. So they may be able to talk with me about a life situation, but how I react and the choices I make determine the eventual outcome. For example, on occasion Laz has cautioned me about situations or people but has never indicated that the result of interacting with these events or people was set in stone. After all, I have free will.

It is rare that a pause occurs in any of my dialogues with Laz, but on one occasion I found an opening and chose to see if I could get a peek into my future. Dangerous as it sounds, I could not resist.

My mother was a fan of buying the *National Enquirer* magazines that hung next to the candy rack as you placed your groceries on the cashier's belt. She would often share what she felt were the most interesting readings with us. One of her favorite purchases was the January edition that proclaimed all the future predictions for the upcoming year by the psychic Jean Dixon. Maybe that is where I developed the curiosity and courage to ask Laz about what would occur in my future. I knew that I needed to frame my question correctly, so I asked the question for myself: What was going to happen for me in the future?

> Bud: Laz can you give me some insight into what might be happening next in my lifetime? The way I currently live, will it be modified?

Laz: Extremely.

B: [*shocked by the immediate response*] In what way?

L: I have taught you that all time is happening now and, because of that, being specific about what will take place becomes difficult. Think about it. What would someone, two hundred years ago, think about your world if they stumbled into it today?

B: Shocked, I would presume.

L: More than that. They would wonder why you let all of this happen and why you did not learn from their time. They would be saddened to see your environment and the destruction of the land. Animals that roamed their world are gone or almost extinct. People no longer join together. Think of the tears they would shed.

B: But with everything that is happening now, I am curious about what might come to pass.

L: You are not hearing me. Change is always happening; nothing is forever. You learned that in Virginia with the holy ones [Thai monks].

B: Yes, I learned about impermanence there, but I remain curious about future events.

Laz isn't dancing around the topic, but he is starting to emphasize that the number of variables that enter into projecting into the future are extraordinary. His comment about "all time is happening now" equates to the concept that all the possible outcomes of the future are available depending on our choices. He has not shut down on this topic—yet—so I continue to pry.

L: Do you think you can change events if I tell you?

B: I wasn't thinking about that. I was actually thinking that there have been writings here about land-mass changes and populations being reduced. Is there truth to that?

L: Earth is a colony, Bud, which you do not know, and they will always need people to jump-start with the knowledge.

B: [*to Shirlet*] I am not going to get an answer, am I?

S: [*smiling*] He is giving you what he feels comfortable with.

B: Laz, will I be here to see any significant changing of the future?

L: Perhaps. That is one possibility.

B: Seriously, is that all you are going to give me on this topic? Would you prefer that I moved on?

L: There is a sad point to this peek you ask. There is a good road and a bad road; the choice will be for all. It all depends on where humanity goes and the choices made. Which one do you want me to share with you?

B: I know you are reluctant to talk about this, but can you discuss the good road?

L: The good road is going back to your roots, but it will have what I have just shared. Believe this or not, this civilization can destroy itself with its technology. With great technology comes great loss. Loss of one's emotional connection, and with that a loss to the ties of your soul. With that will come great danger or, sadly enough, destruction of the populations.

B: Let's talk more about back to the basics; I feel more at ease there.

L: The back to the basics would be without the incredible onslaught of technology that has the capacity of controlling the masses. Back to the basics would be more people living off the land immediately available to them, living in smaller community tribes, and living with others that you trust without question. Having your water. Making it all old-time school, which would make it harder on your human shell because the human shell is not used to that type of work at this stage. Back to the basics would be giving up the reliance on the technology. Your technology has become your prison. Hmm…maybe you would be giving up your prison for freedom. You may see this start to occur. You may be exactly where you are spiritually. If not, as suggested, you may be with me viewing it and feeling sorry for the people.

B: Will both roads be available to us, or is it an all-or-nothing proposition?

L: It is one road or the other; that is why it is so hard to talk about. I can give you more, but it must stay here with you.

At this point Laz asked to have the tape turned off so that he may share more specific information—material that he specifically asked not to have in this writing. His reasons? Too much information from him would deny us the responsibility of making our life and soul choices. On this point he was adamant that he would not give information that would interfere with any choice a soul could make.

My apologies for such a short view and an abrupt end, but Laz shut down, and I think he went further than he had intended. I have so many more questions; maybe another opportunity to ask them will present itself.

Although Laz's picture doesn't necessarily present as picture perfect, he consistently indicates that all of humankind has the power to change events—even the gravest of situations. Whether all of us experience what he has shared remains in our own hands.

I didn't share this to make anyone uncomfortable. To be honest, I wasn't even sure I should include this material. After all, the predictions from the *National Enquirer* that made us nervously laugh as kids just scared us in the end. I thought it was interesting, however, that Laz took the time to speak on the topic. Change is inevitable, and Laz has the capacity to merge that into his personal teaching, whether it is my intimate change or the change around all of us. Modification to the pulsation of human energy, he shared, has the capacity to change anything, positively or negatively, and in this case, changing any course requires an awakening of the human spirit and possibly significant modification to our vibration.

CHAPTER 17

Truth, Dirt, Music, and Angels

When I made the decision to explore the world of soul guides, Shirlet was firm in telling me, "Bud, your guides will only tell you the truth. There will be no hiding. They know you better than you know yourself. So be careful about your decision to link up, and more importantly, think about your questions before you speak. They will not hold anything back, and you have to be prepared for that."

Truth can be elusive; it is so easy for me to hide within a self-created fantasy existence and avoid taking responsibility for my actions. My life seems so much easier when I don't confront the exactness of my existence. I could skate through life and see where it ends, or, like an advanced guide once said, "If you are standing on the edge of a cliff and a hungry T-Rex that hasn't eaten for days is at your back, you can avoid being eaten by stepping over the edge." With no logical alternative presented, I decided it would be best if I mustered the courage to take a leap of faith.

> B: [*to Shirlet*] Once Laz asked, "Can you take the truth and break it into four and tell me what is most accurate?" At the time, I avoided the question because I had no answer. [*to Laz*] Check this out, Laz. I think truth broken into four parts is one, what you think it is; two, what you would like it to be; three, what others think it is; and four, the real truth is what is in your heart.

L: You are correct. Now you know.

B: Because this is such an important part for me, it took time to sort out the message. Once I opened myself up to this, I got insight. Maybe it is energy you gave, Laz; maybe it was more insight. I just started to be different.

L: Think about it. If I put a big mirror in front of you, and you look into it, what is behind it?

B: Is it everything you have been? A totality...

L: Right. A reflection of oneself. There is a time when you would have never known that. You were unaware. Disinterested.

B: That was because I did not have the self-trust to believe.

L: So you tell me. What is your conscious mind connected to? Why is it part of your body, and how can you use it?

B: It is connected to spirit. A little scary because, at times, I feel like I am detaching.

L: That is because you are connecting into our world. Not like a death sentence of your human shell, but a death sentence of your human thought.

B: I have to open up? If I can deal with my fear, the openness allows me to experience a whole different level. [*to Shirlet*] I need to ask Laz for some validation. [*to Laz*] When I ask for white light, I feel a physical sensation over my body. What is that?

L: You should. You are connecting to your aura. I have a question for you. Where did dirt come from?

Now I have had some interesting questions from Laz, but this was the most peculiar. I mean really, Laz, dirt?

[pause]

>Shirlet: That's what he said. I'm just listening. [*with a smile*]

>B: We, as humans, created it?

>L: When?

>B: I don't know...In the beginning?

>L: [*joking*] I didn't see you in the lab. Where did dirt come from?

>B: Did spirit create dirt?

>L: Then what is spirit?

>B: Spirit in total is what we call God.

>L: And what is that?

>B: Part of it is me, because I am a spark of...

>L: You are. And what else?

>B: And everything?

>L: All-consuming. Let me explain. If you have a red rose in your left hand [*pause*], go ahead and look at it. Tell me what it is thinking.

>B: It is thinking, "What will I do with it?"

L: No. What is it thinking?

B: [*long pause*] Do I understand creation?

L: No. It is thinking what you are thinking because you have all-consumed it in your aura. It has become one with you. Tell me this, and you will tell us that you have conquered your limitations. Why is there music?

B: I can tell you what music is for me. I think music is the language of the soul. It is what calms the soul.

L: [*eager*] Go ahead. Keep going.

B: Can I answer in a question? Is it the sound that our vibration level produces?

L: [*excited*] Yes. You are an instrument. Every time you walk, you actually have a vibrational level that plays music. Why do you think that when people are leaving their bodies they hear bells ring and music? It is not just the universe that they are hearing; it is themselves. Your spinal cord has thirty-three rings on it. Like a harp. Like an instrument. When you move, it actually plays music. That is why, when your abilities are developed, if somebody is out of tune because he or she are ill, you or others that are aware will hear it.

B: [*changing topics*] Laz, are you and other guides misinterpreted as guardian angels at times?

L: Yes.

B: Are you, in fact, the guardian angels?

L: No.

B: Do I have a guardian angel who is not you?

L: Yes.

B: Angels have never incarnated?

L: Correct, but we know more of what you are going through because of what we have experienced live there. Not that the angels don't know, because they are many and amazing on all levels of your conscious mind and below; however, we have been through enough to help or guide you in the right direction. That is why we are called soul guides.

B: Will people be confused about what guides like you can do for them and what is destiny and free will?

L: Everything is free will; however, people are not using their free will. People are conditioned to be controlled and their reality reinvented within their minds and the reality that your government and the people who control all of you through that as well. So people are not of free will; therefore, they place themselves more into trouble and are losing their way and losing themselves. The biggest loss any human can take is the losing of self.

B: [*respectfully*] Laz, we never answered where dirt came from. If I was not in the lab, perhaps you were. [*joking*]

L: This is still a good question. I need to ask you some more questions, then. I would like to know from you again, where did dirt come from?

You would think that I would learn. I was home free and about to move on, but, impulsively, I asked again about dirt. Think about it. I had an advanced soul at my disposal and the ability to ask any questions about human existence, and I asked repeatedly about dirt. If I had known that earth science would be on the exam, I would have studied more. I was about to look foolish...again.

B: Let's move on instead. [*laughing*]

DIRT, TRUTH, MUSIC AND BUNGEE CORDS

L: No. I do not wish to move on. That is a loaded question. Let's get started. I am going to school you, and we are going to answer your pressing question together. Again, you tell me where you think dirt came from.

B: But, Laz, we have already gone through this. We did...

L: The position that you put us in is a stroll down the path of a hill. We are going to go on that path. [*smiling*] Dirt? Hmm...What are the components of dirt?

B: Components?

L: Yes.

B: I don't know. Any number of minerals?

L: What are they?

B: [*guessing*] Atoms? Energy?

L: So what is your answer?

I didn't really have a clue at this point, but I did know that we are made up of energy. So assuming the T-Rex was approaching from the rear, I leaped over the cliff again.

B: I am dirt. [*laughing*]

L: [*laughing*] Who created it?

B: Our father, the creator?

L: Who created our father, our source?

B: [*confused*] That question is beyond me.

L: Everything is energy, vibration, frequency. It is all corresponding in an overall hue of creating eventful connections. Hmm…I would say that obviously our creator, who is one and all and as we are one and all, created it. I also say it was created from energy. And it is. Now what do you think?

B: The human terms would be that God created all the energy?

L: Some would say that is very true, and I would be one of them. Some would say then who is God? And when that question is asked, you have to go into a timeless abyss of high electrical magnetic frequency, a level of hertz (kHz) people never suspected exist. The planet is a living organism, and it fires energy, and it has dirt. Hmm…so your answer, if you really think about it, would be correct. You are dirt. You are water. You are beautiful air. You are fire. You are frequency. You are a creation of knowledge far beyond and above anything that could be comprehensible by a human mind at this point in evolution.

Truth, dirt, music, and angels, all in the matter of a few minutes. What better learning lab could I ask for? There were times when I would walk away from some sessions wondering who was more scattered, me or Laz. In the end, however, every item he discussed with me would come full circle as he made his points regarding my development. So I am sure that many of these subjects will return as lessons in the future. This was a surprise pop quiz. I needed to either study harder or stop asking so many damn questions. Time and again I am reminded that the entity that I am interacting with knows me extremely well and is only ever truthful, regardless of how I feel about the topic or the energy giving the answer. The truth about who I am, or who we are, is such a delicate place to venture. Laz is trying to get me there, and the path is increasingly funky. I wondered what the next topic would be and when he would spring the next pop quiz.

CHAPTER 18

Feedback from Laz

I remember reading once that, during an afterlife review, a soul's senior council member asked which life event was the most memorable and positive in terms of its soul growth. As I recall, the soul thought for many moments and then recounted that he had been very successful in that life by providing jobs and security for many during the Depression. With the other council members waiting, the original questioner referred to the time the soul had missed his bus and sat next to a woman who was crying. He reassured her that everything was going to be just fine and then jumped on the next available bus for work. The soul was shocked that such a small act had made such a big impact on his council. Well, I received the same lesson one evening when the conversation turned to current life accomplishments. Like the soul in the story, I was equally surprised at the answer.

> Laz: Let me ask you another question since we are on this conversational track.
>
> Ucerous: I have one also.
>
> L: I need to know this. You tell me what you have learned the most of me, from me, as of me. I am above you and so below you as you have learned with the extensions of the energy I have given you to do and trust into learning—

Shirlet tries to interrupt this run-on sentence.

Shirlet: What he is asking, of all the things he has asked you to do, which one hit you the most?

Bud: Which homework assignment?

S: Yes.

B: Interesting. I gravitate to the most recent year. The one I found most immediate learning was the tree, hill, and water. It was an immediate learning of where I was as opposed to where I thought I was. Also there was the rose that taught me that everything you touch becomes part of your essence. Your aura.

L: You have learned well from me. The one that I can see that I have to give you gratitude for is saving the tree that was being persecuted by the other trees.

Very early in my discussions with Laz, he had asked whether I could differentiate between a male and female tree. Peculiar, right? Not being a tree hugger, I did not know the difference. He said I should place my left hand (the heart hand) on the trunk of the tree and tell him what I felt and what my instincts were. OK, I thought. I can give anything a chance once. After all, here I am talking to guides.

I went to a beautiful bike park where I often ran. As I entered the trails and the race macadam, there were hundreds of trees. I first tried at the entrance, when no one was watching, with a pine tree that was losing sap. His name was Honor. The feeling I received when I touched him was that he was sick and afraid of falling in the strong winds.

Farther down the trail was a tree with a crooked trunk. It was right at the entrance to the bike trails. Placing my left hand on the trunk, I got the immediate sensation of being female and ugly. Further, I got the impression that the other trees surrounding her were not friendly to her. I felt the emotion deeply and thought to myself, in the hope that the tree would pick up the message, that I was there to rename her. I told her and the others that going forward she was to be referred to as Bella, meaning "beauty," and that she was to be treated differently. I visit both Bella and Honor whenever I go to the trail for a run.

B: That is interesting that you say that.

L: Do you know how grateful she truly is? She thinks about you constantly and owes you and feels a need to tell you. Just thought you should know that.

U: I have a question. Are you ready for this one? You tell me how you can be kinder to yourself.

B: [*pausing*] There are three things that tie together. One is to be less analytical. To do that I have to be more disciplined, which actually sounds like a contradiction. The biggest thing I have to learn is to forgive myself.

U: Can I ask you a question? Do you know your answers are always between the lines, not the lines you seek or gravitate to or from? How do you not know that?

B: You mean indecisive?

S: Bud, he is saying you are not connecting to get the right things from yourself.

U: Too analytical. I would think so. Maybe a rush of thought that really leads nowhere, like a river with no substance. Tell me one thing you have done for yourself in the last seven days that was kind to your body, soul, and mind? Something that brings you joy and substance?

B: I haven't done anything.

U: Let me ask you something. You have been given a vessel, an incredible vessel to be on this planet. Given to accomplish a view that is an amazing view and work that you could be remembered for; however, you are not kind to your vessel. Why is that? What is missing?

B: What is getting in the way is my trying to control everything.

U: When is the last time you did something without thinking it over and thinking yourself out of it? Something that would be a pleasure to your mind, body, and soul?

B: It has been a very long time.

U: Give me the reason.

B: Trying to control situations or emotions or people around me. Trying to keep everything harmonious.

L: Let me come into this and help Ucerous and pull this to a better issue. OK, I want you to do something for me. I want you to hold up your hands. Now I want you to pretend that you have the world in both hands, and there is a planet in both hands the size of your palm. There are little people in it who are great visionaries. There are animals, beauty and flowers, trees and earth. It is your decision what will happen to these planets. So you are to keep an eye on them and care for them. Let's just take your left hand, and I want you to just turn it over. Where is that planet now, Bud?

B: It is gone.

L: Why did that happen?

B: Because I did what you asked me to do.

L: Hmm, so you just listened to others and let a whole universe and people perish at the thought of a whim. You did not stand up for them and try to save them. So let's just see about this. This is you, and you have totally let yourself go.

B: I understand what you are saying. I don't stand up for what I believe in consistently. Am I right?

L: Totally right. You also don't pamper your shell. When was the last time you took yourself somewhere that was just fun? Where you did not have to control something or someone, did not have to analyze something, had to do nothing?

B: Been a long time.

L: I have something for you, then. And I want it done. Within the next two weeks, I want you to take yourself to an amusement park, any of your choosing. I want you to walk around, enjoy the people, and not analyze them. I want you to eat ice cream or anything you want and have a good time, and when you go to your car, I want you to tell me what you learned.

B: OK. [*to Shirlei*] The irony of holding the worlds. After all my discussions with them, I didn't think of questioning it.

L: What I am trying to show you is that, in the mist, there are humans who do not question what other humans tell them to do, whether right or wrong.

B: I just assumed that because it was you, Laz...

S: But that is the lesson.

B: Another way of describing what Ucerous was talking about is that I could do more if I were truthful with myself and what I really believe in and stand up for. And if I make any of this public, I better be prepared because I will get questions to inquire about my internal belief by people whose intention is to disprove U and Laz exist.

U: So be kind to yourself. Go to the amusement park, and have a good time. Make sure you remember how to smile without having to for a reason. Oh! And you have to be there for a while. You can't just go in and turn around and leave.

It's rare that I stop and take a moment to think about the impact that I have on other people and things in the course of the day, but I do have an impact, as does everyone. As Laz was speaking, I reflected on times when I'd been completely inappropriate and not as helpful as he suggested I was with the tree, Bella. I have those bad days, being cut off while driving or pushed aside at the grocery store, as I suspect we all do. It's interesting to have a spiritual review after such actions. I can see my spiritual council going overtime on just a few habitual acts of unkindness I have mastered over my time here. However, once these actions are brought to my awareness, my approach changes radically. If I have the capacity to change the vibration and energy of a tree, imagine what we can do for one another. I think about that more often now and reflect daily during meditation about my impact within the world that I move in. I try now to take a silent pause when I have the instinct to react, a skill I learned at the monastery. This has helped but has not completely removed the impulse to react without thinking. On this matter, I am still a work in progress.

A deceased friend Dr. Tony Crane used to write notes to the schools that his two sons attended, saying, "Anthony and Matthew cannot attend school today because we are enjoying a day of joy and happiness." Simply put, U and Laz are telling me to venture to the amusement park and have a day of personal joy and happiness. In the midst of my transformation, Laz and U are reminding me to attend to myself. This has as much of an impact as attending to others. Laz did not use the word *balance*, but that was the takeaway from the evening's discussion.

CHAPTER 19

Changing Emotional Healing:

I have been working in the psychiatric industry for over forty years, both as a clinician and later as a senior health-care executive. During that time I have witnessed the transition from the traditional approaches of psychoanalysis to a wide variety of therapeutic interventions, including the revolution of psychotropic medications. Along the way I studied and my industry experienced the introduction of theories by Alfred Adler, Abraham Maslow, Harry Stack Sullivan, and many, many more, always with the good intention of addressing the whole individual: mind, body, and soul.

Unfortunately, my observations are that we have concentrated heavily on the symptoms associated with the mind and body, often at the expense of the spiritual portion of the individual. In many behavioral health facilities I have operated, spiritual programs consist of having outside clergy visit when appropriate. Most treatment teams would authorize this but typically only on a case-by-case basis and not as an integrated program component.

I mention this not as a criticism but as a prelude to my involvement and interest in the spiritual development of people facing difficult challenges, including myself. It is not something that I consciously chose; I was guided to this place.

Sadly, even with the revolution in the manufacturing and distribution of psychotropic medications, we continue to struggle with the societal impact of an increasing number of citizens becoming handicapped mentally, physically, and spiritually. Additionally, we are also experiencing the influence legally with an increase in violence and arrests being made directly as a result of untreated psychological conditions. Most disappointing to me, however, is the slow inclusion of an integrated medical and psychological approach to the overall treatment of these personal trials, specifically the absence of a consistent approach of self-healing, working together with our industry-accepted best practices.

With Laz and U advising me as to how to find the ideal working environment, I decided to present a question about their observations, hoping to get a peek into their view on changes in the mental health field. After all, Laz had once suggested that many components of both physical and mental confrontations are stress driven and that any distinct depression or anxiety is no different than any I would encounter if I went into the next twenty houses on Shirlet's block.

> Bud: Laz, what needs to change for us to really become the healers that we need to be in the areas of treating people we presume have a mental illness?
>
> Laz: Belief.
>
> B: Belief in what?
>
> L: Belief that it can change. Most people have a belief system that once you have it, you have to continue it. Don't you know that across your planet, they lock people up for that and never try to help them? With that, they can actually destroy the brain, put them away, and feed them once in a while to keep their shell alive and get the monies. It has to be a belief system. Not only does it have to be that, the other way is *involvement*. People are not involved in shaping the system on your planet, and it will stay the same. Sadly enough, your drug administration runs your planet, and it is a money opportunity. It will always keep mental illness on an above and top level because it is one of their top-paying subjects. So that will have to change. *Known* is another word I would like to put in there. Do

you know a lot of people who they assume have mental illness do not, and many people who don't, actually do? I don't think they all really know. It is like a Cracker Jack box, and they are pulling out the prize, and it may or may not be. Obviously you are aware of this as most in the field are.

B: Is that why I am so discouraged by the field I chose to be in?

L: People will say Shirlet is crazy. But she is not. She is just highly psychic and more open to the energies that we present to her and to others. Sadly enough, I feel that there are many in her position, maybe not in her ability, but still in her position, that really do not have a mental illness.

B: So all thought creates solid form, which is what you teach. If it is already out there in the universe that a person is mentally ill, that categorizes that person. Now we have to reduce the symptoms of this, and the one way to do that is we will create a drug that will control the symptoms.

L: Let me inject here. You are answering your own question. Think about it. Once drug companies have created that substance [drug], and they keep people in a dependent position and the universe still thinks that they are mentally ill; that is why they are taking care of just the symptoms. They know that. Think about it.

B: Help me out, Laz. Take me twenty years into the future. How are we dealing with this issue if we do not break this cycle? What do we need to break so that people begin to heal with the essence of the individual?

L: Bring down the house of cards that has put them in that position in the first place. Instead of taking them to a healer, and the healer taking them to a mental facility for "nuts," as they would call them, which continually keeps them on the mental-illness, low profile frequency, they need to be taken to a healer and to a different

CHANGING EMOTIONAL HEALING:

healing facility. The name has to change, thus changing the frequency. You know that words carry frequency and can damage or heal. That needs to be a change as well.

B: Take it one step further. What is it that they would be doing in a healing environment? What would be different from the apparent insanity that we created with the current approach?

L: Having a substance of love, hope, and abundance. Let me specialize you in this. They would be having people who understood them instead of putting them on a drug and saying they are insane and putting them in a facility and locked somewhere. They would have people around the clock working with them to get them through their anxieties they were experiencing. They would be having professionals there to counsel them to see if they were psychic. Focusing on what started their condition. To see if there is some chemical imbalance or just something being done by spirits by means of an illusion. They will have all the proper healers, physicians, and people around them that are needed, hence not what is happening now. They would be teaching how to self-heal.

B: What would it be called, if not mental illness? What is the word?

L: The word doesn't exist. There is no name to give it except that it is the process of healing and hope. *Healing* would be the healing of the brain, and *hope* would be the hope of it staying that way. I think it is incumbent on you to look at it on a different level. Healing is a whole different word energy level to make a person better.

B: If all conditions were right, is this something that could really happen?

L: Yes. Why doesn't it become a process of healing the mind, which would be the opposite of mental illness? The word *mental illness* strikes up a lower vibration to say that you are mentally ill and there is no hope for you because there is nothing in the word that says you will get better, is there?

B: No. Just that you are dysfunctional.

L: You have been put into a category, and that is where you stay.

B: And that feeds the public image?

L: Think about it. Say a mental facility was building a place by your house. What would the community say? They would be saying the mental illness is coming to destroy our property. They would be terrified and running and moving. But think if a healing-mind facility was being built with all the professional healers we discussed. That would conjure maybe awareness, curiosity, and maybe wanting to help. Different, isn't it? But you already know this.

B: So, once again, like you have been saying earlier, if you project an image that is built upon negative energy, it will draw more negative energy into it.

L: It will never end. You will have to change the face and the image. At this stage, where is it at? It is about money. How many times have you heard "no money, no mission"? Saying that, where is the energy going? Healing? I don't think so. The human mind is quite powerful. If anyone can stop you from using it and letting it heal itself and do what it needs to do, obviously that will happen.

B: And it keeps what we have identified as the outliers out of the mainstream. Laz, if the like-minded created the healing environments, could they learn to heal themselves?

L: So true. They learn to heal despite everything else. The environments that are created will play a big role in all this.

There it is: my soul guides' initial impressions on how we as a human species can start creating a process to self-heal. I feel sad every time I revisit this discussion. I have been as guilty as any other in focusing, sometimes exclusively, on the financial business of treating individuals with these challenges. The question at this time is whether we are content with our processes and the outcomes of our treatment systems. If not, what are we as professionals going to do to change our approaches? Apparently, from Laz's perspective, ignoring the environmental energy that we create works in such a way as to prohibit the course of healing. All the stakeholders associated with emotional restoration would need to be active in establishing a like-minded approach if "hopeful healing" is to have a chance. Perhaps time will tell. If not, certainly the continuation of our current industry outcomes will.

It's very difficult to change the cycle of professional behaviors. Perhaps that is why Laz suggested taking down the house of cards. Mental health professionals have a vested interest in maintaining our treatment systems and approaches; after all, many of our egos and finances are identified through those historical methods. New interpersonal styles of approaching individuals, mass-produced instructional recordings, and professional conferences all seemingly end in the same place, with very little change. Laz and U maintain that the power of the mind is enormous and that the capacity is there to heal. Finding our way there would be an extraordinary journey.

CHAPTER 20

Faith, Hope, and Belief

U would say that confidence is something that can vacillate depending on the fragility of the human ego, and I was not exempt from that, in particular while my life was under review by both of my guides. Confronting the fact that I had been less than truthful about my life was…daunting to say the least. Changing in such a way that I was able to accept the accuracy of my being was going to require extraordinary courage, and, as a result, I found myself looking for hope. Truth is so complex; it involves my character, my values, and my authentic beliefs about my world and all the people in it. Confronting core certainties has the potential to give me a brain freeze. I was hoping that Laz would have something to say for me and all of us on the matter of belief. After all, the Thai monks indicated that I am but an accumulation of stored, generally unchallenged principles. The only remaining question was how Laz and U were going to confront those beliefs.

Laz: Like I said, let's talk about free will from my point of view while we are here. What do you think I am going to say?

Bud: I wasn't prepared for this, but…

L: You should be prepared because I am always with you. Don't you sense my energy everywhere?

B: I was sensing you on the drive over and trying to listen.

L: And? Have you learned anything?

B: Don't pick on me. [*laughing*] I think my free will is often inhibited because of my state of mind or obsession with things that scatter my mind.

L: I was going to say that you have two sides of your brain. One side is productive, and the other is unproductive. Who do you think is winning?

B: Cleary the unproductive.

L: You are starting to second-guess your best work. Why?

B: I'm not sure that is true.

L: From that time I talked with you…what you called "the beatdown."

B: That time we talked, it was about core beliefs and articulating them in a real sense.

L: Why do you think that you need to have a fantasy in your considerations when reality is what is really about the work?

B: I think I am over that.

L: I think that your writing can be quite a success, despite that it has taken you eons.

B: Despite the beatdown? [*laughing*]

L: Tell me the end result of the writing.

B: There are three. First, is for me to face the truth about me. It wasn't what I expected when we started this but you have taught me that it is the most important. The second is legitimately getting the soul

L: guide relationship in the public domain so that people know that they exist. And third, breaking apart the life fantasy I had created.

L: Can you put that in one word?

B: [*pause*] Open?

L: Faith. You have to explore and give humanity faith so that they can continue to talk and approach this on a different level. So that they can have sessions with their soul guides. So they can have sessions with those who love them and are around them. So they can talk to them someday. Communicate with them, even on their own. Faith.

B: In order to make that real for them to do, I have to get myself to a place where I can have direct communication with you to demonstrate that it is possible?

L: You have to take baby steps. You are only at step one. First you have to make it real for them, which will change that. If you continue to make all writing about realism and what is really happening, then they will see their lives on a real level. And then you can continue to write in the future of how you have progressed. That will give hope to talk to their soul guides. The caution to this tale, however, is you have to remember to keep stepping up and not go down.

[pause]

L: The lake will help you when the time comes. The water gives you power. In the future, you will buy a house on a lake. It will be beautiful, and it will have a view over the lake that will be your office. That will empower us for communication and empower you to be lost in the communication.

B: That's cool. [*joking with Shirlet*] Want to come?

Shirlet: Beautiful.

B: Last night I was sitting behind my house with my brother, and I shared with him some of our discussions. He was saying that the writing should exclusively be about my adventure with you, Laz.

L: Why do you think you are here?

B: [*lightheartedly*] I also told my brother that I have to be careful about the questions that I ask because you are very literal.

S: Extremely.

L: I will not be the only one talking with you. Ucerous is here.

B: I have to apologize to you, Ucerous, for suggesting in the past that all of this is entertainment.

Ucerous: I will ask you a question, but first I want to know what you ask me first.

S: You are going to get two different points of view tonight.

B: And they are different. I started a couple of weeks ago asking different people, "If you had the opportunity to ask your guide a question, what would you ask?" and I got across-the-board responses.

Both: We know.

B: I am sure you do. I was given everything from "Can they solve my ancestry.com problems?" to things more serious. One that was interesting to me was, "What is the purpose of humankind right now, in this period of time we are living in? What is the purpose of all this?"

L: Creation and feeling. One cannot exist without the other. You are in the process of forming a creation you are part of. You have to keep creating life, or life will take a different form and subdivide itself and not have this form. All life is happening now, and all form is happening now. When there are very many dimensional levels, we are creating because the mind is that powerful; however, most people are creating a lot of strife and pain. This subject is a problem, not just on this planet, but the other surrounding universal territories as well. We are all to be of creation so we can continue to make other universes, which again is a form of creation, and we are from that form.

B: Is that like saying if we have a negative process that we are creating, we are feeding that, and it grows?

L: Consider it a junkyard dog. I will put it in terms that you are able to understand. Say you are at your house, and you have a neighbor who has a junkyard dog, and every day he goes out and beats it and then gives it food and makes it attack other people and then gives it treats. Obviously the dog will get more negative and more aggressive and want to harm someone. Unfortunately, Bud, your species is not different from that conception or possibility.

B: Feed the anger and it gets bigger and starts to bring other negative energies.

S: It can become a monster.

B: If the word is *creation*, can I assume that we are not doing a very good job with that now? Is there something that we can all do to move it to something more positive?

L: Again, the word is *faith*. Humans do not have faith in themselves. Will not have faith in their future and therefore care not about it. If a human does not care about the future, then he or she does not care about cause and effect. Therefore, he or she does not care about what he or she does to humankind or other living substances.

B: If we restated the intention of our discussion to mean a small step to start to establish faith…that faith comes in the form of the resources available to us that instill a different sense of faith in us.

L: The faith has always been there. You have to give someone hope, or should I say something to look forward to. If a human has something to look forward to…Say a child down the street is looking forward to the fair. He can't wait for all the rides and to get his cotton candy and his candy apples. He is going to do everything he can if his mother says he must clean the house or he does not go. He has something to look forward to. Unfortunately, humankind has nothing to look forward to. All you see on your television scope is war, threat of war, implacable substances with fire damage, murder, and rape. Another thing, humans are visualizing and controlling and are bringing storms and violence to this planet. It's almost become a human frenzy. All humans want this to happen, and they are looking forward to a storm to end our beautiful world. How sad it has come that humankind has no building block for creation and nature to thrive and have decided to bring it down.

B: Are we giving up? Is that accurate?

L: No. They are being told to, and they are being beat down by poverty and have nothing to look forward to because one of the gods you have created is the god of substance, money.

S: He is very good and smart.

B: Is the better word *hope* or *faith*?

L: The word needs to be *faith* because there is no hope without faith.

B: Must believe in something? Is there a growing percentage of the population that is ready to hear this kind of message from guides like you, or is it still…?

L: Your answer is no. They are not ready, but they need to be. There is a sense of urgency. I would have never pushed for this if I didn't see and know it.

B: Laz, if we had ten people, how many would believe in what you just said?

L: Three. But they would tell ten who would produce three more and so on. If we save one person on this planet, it is all worth something. Everything we discuss is like a how-to discussion. How to save life and the planet's life. Think about it.

Over the years, both Laz and Ucerous have peppered their discussions with an emphasis on the consistency of my belief systems, and this session was the first that transcended me personally. In reflection, it is such a simple concept that faith equals hope. Coupled with the notion that all thought creates solid form, I could be creating my own negative intention. Knowing both of these guides, I suppose that breaking down the negative personal practices that I possess is the key to change. On a larger scale, Laz does not think we have much to look forward to; however, there is reason for optimism. He suggests that we all clean our own rooms so we have the opportunity to enjoy cotton candy at the fair. Despite the fun analogy, I take that seriously. Faith and hope rarely come up in my daily discussions, yet as Laz is suggesting, they are the core of what drives me on a daily basis. When I have taken the time to ask others what they hoped for the future, they would ring out with large-scale ideas, like world peace. When queried, however, about their personal status, they were often left hollow and requested more time to think about it. I take the time now to better understand my own response to these questions because in the answer lies the foundation of my own truth.

CHAPTER 21

What Laz and Ucerous Really Think

Laz sometimes lowers his teaching/learning shield and becomes more, dare I say, humanlike, whereas Ucerous tends to remain very serious minded and stoic. I had one instance, however, when both were willing to share their personal opinions on what others might want to know about working with soul guides. The glow of their light was off me for a fraction of a moment, and I took the opportunity, knowing that it was happening because they wished it, not because I could manipulate them or the discussion topics. Along with my internal sigh of relief, here is a brief excerpt of their personal thoughts.

> Bud: What is one topic that is of importance, which I have not covered and that is needed to be known?
>
> Laz: I think the best one is what people don't see that is around them. It is really there. The beauty of the planet. Creation is happening around them, whether it is a snail being born or a dauphin being born or a beautiful bird flying and taking care of its nest. What is happening around them in a positive way is what they never look at and see. Do you know how many lives it would save that maybe wanted to die that day if they only knew how much life

was being born around them? They would want to be part of it. Show them there is a bigger plan here and that they are a part of that plan. This has to be part of your message.

B: If we had everyone in this room and wanted to give them one thing that they could do that would help raise the awareness so that they would understand, what would you recommend?

L: Go outside. Pick a flower. Smell it, and look at every detail of the petals. How amazing it is that something created that.

B: Increase the awareness of what is really created?

L: Yes. You and they are part of that as well.

Laz looks for the simplest positive response, exploring the helpful possibilities of the human condition and encouraging the bright side of what is available to us. Ucerous is more pragmatic, as previously discussed, and extremely straightforward. His response gave a different perspective to the question.

B: Ucerous, do you have one thing that we have yet to cover or that is critical to know?

Ucerous: Yes. The dark side of all things. They can learn to prevent it and get around it and not fall into it.

B: Will that scare people? It certainly scares me.

U: No. It is realism. We have to tell the truth. There will be many people who may read what you write and wonder why there are murders every day. Many people wondering why their house is burning down. Or why tornadoes are killing their families and no god is stopping it. There will be people saying, "Why can't I get a hold of my son who died? I loved him so much. Why can't I hear him?" This is very important.

B: What is the learning that is needed about this? Is it simply that there are soul paths that need to be completed?

U: That is correct but only a small part of it. The answer is thought creates solid form. If you and ten thousand people are watching TV and they are showing a tornado hitting Kansas, all those people concentrate on that all week. You can bet that in a couple of months, if not sooner, a tornado will hit Kansas. You cannot break through solid form and stop creation.

B: That works both ways. If something is positive...

U: Yes. Show me five houses that are thinking something positive right now. Most people are thinking of the bills or losing their home or a bad relationship. Their jobs are bad, and they have no knowledge of anything other than loss. They are creating more loss. The more they sit and stare at the bills, the more that comes to them. The more they think about the man who is hitting them, of the drunk in their bed who they thought was a good man, the more they are bringing the next man to do the same thing. It is always creation. We cannot and do not get involved in creation. We can try to help or maybe help to see things differently to create a different scenario, but most of you will not listen or cannot listen.

B: But if they had the capacity to listen, then they would have the ability to short-circuit what you are talking about, correct?

U: There would never be a war again.

B: Unbelievable. We are back to faith and hope.

U: Consumption creates consumption.

B: What can you recommend to people that would help to break this down?

U: We could use the old adage that the church has been using on people for years. Take a page out of their book. Very simple. What do the church people on TV preach to people? They yell, "Send us some money, and money will come to you. Send us money, and your bills will be paid. God will bless you because you send us money." Hmm, I think they know all about all thought creating solid form. It isn't about sending them money. It is that you think that you are going to get something from it so you created the endeavor. You brought it. They have to change their minds.

B: What would have been a better thing for the church to say?

U: Believe in yourself. You are already blessed. Believe in yourself. This is all about giving people hope to make the changes so they can change the world, and they can help themselves. They will be able to do something that will involve creation that is actually positive. I am very tired of going by houses and hearing everybody say that they can't wait for the end of the planet. How sad, sick, and twisted they have become to even consider something so horrific.

B: Are they giving up?

U: They are looking for adventures or something that they think would be incredible to happen and be a part of, but why would somebody be a part of destruction? Why not be part of giving birth to a new planet? A new world? A new society with a thought pattern? Why not that?

B: When I refer to the dark side, what is a way of explaining that so that people will not be scared?

U: Describe it as the position we are in at this moment.

Shirlet: Lights out; he's gone.

After this discussion, and throughout the long drive home, I kept thinking about U's comments, about how simple the correction is, yet how impossible it might be considering the conditions in which we all live.

I turned on the radio and was confronted with world affairs as ISIS continued its brutal invasion of the Middle East. How unfortunate it is that U's perception is accurate, and yet the corrective answer lies in all of us. The soul guides are willing to assist, and maybe that is the driving force behind their wanting me to make sure we are all aware of their existence. At the core of their truth, they are trying to help us create a plan to avoid our own destruction. Tough job, but these two have leaped headfirst into the pool with me, and I am thankful for that.

CHAPTER 22

Broken-Glass Souls

Creation and the big bang are the modern-day versions of how it all began—gases exploding, searing matter traveling at astronomical speed until it slows and cools just long enough to construct one universe after another.

Energy, we are told, comes together in multiple forms to fashion what we see, feel, touch, and taste during the course of our lives. But what of us? The essence of what we truly are? How did we come to be—not in this solid human form but in the configuration of what we call our soul?

My interest started when I was confronted with an advanced soul guide named Kadecious. He referred to himself during our very first meeting as having been "polylistically" formed. I wasn't astute enough at the time to pursue the definition or discover if it was even a real word, but I was curious about what he meant by it. I thought that Laz would give me the insight to properly define the term and maybe resolve my chronic inquisitiveness. I expected Laz to provide a complete account of master souls, their roles, and how our souls all came to be born from the source, the essence he calls the father.

> Bud: Laz, a guide named Kadecious used a term that I have been unable to find. Can you tell me what "polylistically formed" means? Is it a multiple version of different souls or multiple versions of the same soul?
>
> Laz: Both. We all are.

B: [*confused*] You need to explain that to me.

L: Think of it this way. Think if you had a glass vase, and you took a hammer and smashed it. Think of all the glass flying all over in shards and pieces. If you had the power, which our father does, you could create all those shards and pieces back into that vase. Now think of this. Think of fractured souls, other souls that may have been fractured, who actually tried to save others or even at my level. Think of them coming together as one great soul. Created to do the work of an army. Then we would have what you are talking about.

B: Would a human like…Gandhi, could that have been a polylistically formed soul coming into existence?

L: Yes. But he was not.

B: Let me ask you a sensitive question.

L: [*smiling*] I am holding onto the arm of my chair.

B: Are there master souls and could they have been mistaken for souls that are polylistically formed?

L: Oh no! They are above that. They would have been the ones to create polylistic souls. Not with their human form, but with their soul forms, which are two different things. A "master soul" would be a good human term to describe them. We have been recreated and recreated by each other, whereas they were created out of the father's hand, and that is where it ended for them.

B: So, we are…[*thinking for a moment*] a mutt? [*chuckling*]

L: That is a good way to put it. Master souls would have been purebred with the powers and energy to do some amazing things.

B: Laz, because the spirit realm is so very complex with all these different entities and levels of souls, when people pass does that make it confusing for them?

L: Depending where they end up. Yes. As I taught you, it all depends on their vibration.

B: Would the father or creator ever allow a soul to be terrified because of the confusion, and would a soul be able to correct those feelings?

L: You can. Let's go back to the tree incident on the bike path. When you approached the trees, and you saw that one was deformed, and you asked the others not to make fun of her, and she started to correct herself better, and they responded differently, she wanted it. You cannot correct anything if someone does not want it. Sometimes there are many beings and others who want to pull into the energy and try to correct it, but the person does not want to change.

B: Is the ultimate end game that we all come together as one energy and unify with the father?

L: You were from that energy field so ultimately we may; however, energy changes and shifts and moves.

B: But still, isn't the goal to explore, grow, and return to the source?

L: We all have many shells, my friend, not just this one. Take the Jurassic period, where the dinosaurs roamed. We were part of that creation process. We have been in shells of different creations on this planet. There were giants that ruled this planet at one time, and we were in those shells as well. The soul has changed and evolved, and if the corresponding soul wanted to participate in the alignment, it could. I think we need to go back to the vase again to make you understand. Consider the beautiful vase again, and that is the ultimate soul—God, if you wish. Consider the hammer hitting it. They are the souls that he has created from himself. You were created out of likeness. Remember that, and all humans have advanced into a pattern now. And consider that you have the shards of glass, and you are hitting them again, and they are created. It keeps going and going, over and over. But at one turn or another, they get further from the creator, and then that is when issues start.

B: Laz, there is an author here, Michael Newton, who references the color of souls. On the outer-edge shards, he writes the color is very white, representing the innocence of a very young soul. The closer you get to the father, there are variations of color, eventually deep purple. Is that a good representation of what you just said but with color?

L: Yes.

B: So the further out, the younger the soul?

L: Yes.

B: And like any youngster, they can be mischievous, adventurous, or misdirected?

L: In some cases, and in others, they are not all young souls. Some souls do not see things as they should as far as pain and suffering. You have many examples of that on your planet where the intention was correct but the ego destroyed anything positive.

There is so much to this topic and many more questions to ask both of Laz and U to get to the finer details of what happens after life. What Laz gave during this exchange was more than I'd anticipated. Frankly, it gave me heartburn as I drove home. It is a uncommon occasion when he ventures away from the a particular teaching/learning moment. I know that I will revisit this area with him again, but I also know that he has something in store for me as well. I have never had a topic of discussion that simply stopped with my questioning. Laz and U always take my inquisitions and turn them back to my life task and the expected accomplishments of my soul. So I will wait in anticipation of what will come and in doing so pull together all my other questions in the hope of getting to the bottom of my curiosity about my creation and ultimately my soul's truth.

There seem to be some common threads in Laz's discussion about the creation when compared to other writings or interpretations. Perhaps the same source is influencing how the versions are constructed. What I find somewhat different is the guide's explanation that there are multiple possible variations of the path each soul can take when reacting to the creation. From Laz's point of view, there is nothing static about a universe made up of energy because it is inhabited by us—souls who have free will.

CHAPTER 23

Describing the World Where Laz Lives

In deciding to take this great adventure with these soul guides, I read and tried to digest as much as I could about the world where they might reside. Perhaps that was the reason I insisted on asking so many trivial questions that both Laz and U would eventually and gracefully answer.

Despite learning who these personalities were, I remained curious about what it would be like "over there," the place where they resided and called home. As I was raised under Catholic dogma, there is certainly a picture in my mind's eye of their place, which I would describe by and large as Christian. After months of discussion, I was sure the image would be adjusted if I ever had the courage to ask.

The poet Dorothy Parker once said that the cure for boredom is curiosity. So to keep my boredom at bay, I simply asked my questions. Dorothy Parker also stated that there was no cure for curiosity.

Bud: Laz, can you describe what it is like to be in the spirit world?

Laz: Which one?

B: Are there multiple levels of the spirit world?

L: Yes. So which one?

B: Can you describe the level where you exist?

L: I exist in consciousness. I exist in light. I exist in a higher frequency. I exist in a frequency of knowing knowledge and participation and freedom of knowledge—that knowledge which is able to help someone or show how to help someone. I exist in knowledge of love not based on fear. I exist in the knowledge of kindness, empathy not based on sorrow or pain. My frequency is much different.

B: Is there a place where this frequency happens, and are there others who are like-minded who exist there?

L: Very much so. I exist in a dimension. I exist in a level of a dimension. I exist in a vibration of a level of a dimension. Think of this, Bud. Think of looking out a screen door. When you look at that screen, see how it is made, and see every little square. Consider this and consider everywhere you look there are screens around you with those squares being a world or a dimension. This is how many you are looking at.

B: That is a thought-provoking way of looking at it. So there is a number that is probably not imagined?

L: When Shirlet says anything can appear in front of you and that it exists, her knowledge of that is correct. As I have come through and truly exist. As you are here in this dimension and truly exist. So there are many other beings that truly exist; whether they are the creation of a positive or negative frequency has yet to be determined. But that does not keep them from existing.

B: Laz, if you and I are mates there, do I exist in the same square of the screen?

L: Very good. Yes. When you are not pulled down in your dimension level within your shell.

B: Depending on what I do here, I could end up in any portion of the screen?

L: If you only knew how many, yes.

B: Is that why you are so intense with me in getting my life together so that I may stay in that portion of the screen?

L: To ascend to us is to be with us. You have to create an energy field that will attract that ascension, meaning vibration. When people pass, depending on what is happening with them, depending on what their vibration is, that determines where they end up. Why do you think some spirits are here against their will but keep haunting? I'll use that word even though it is not a word we use, but you should be able to understand it. There are locations where few adapt to sadness or the pain of how they ceased to exist in a human shell of that time frame and matter. They are pulled into that vibration. Why do you think some people experience what some people term as a hell? They are pulled into that vibration. That was the vibration that they were putting out at the time of their dimensional existence. Why do you think people go to what they term a heaven? They are pulled to that vibration. For you to ascend to the particular position that we are in, you have to considerably raise your vibration.

B: You are referring to the vibration that you are creating during the totality of your existence, correct?

L: It is what you are putting out while you are here. Sadly enough, that is why some do not see their family or loved ones when they pass. It isn't that they didn't want to. Their vibration level puts them in a different dimensional frame. As I said, there are too many dimensions to mention.

B: Once there and in that different vibrational frame, can they work to get to a plane to see their family?

L: Not all. Some, if it is a positive vibrational frame. Once on a lower-vibrational frame, some souls are stuck or lost.

B: Once stuck, does that soul have to come back into another incarnation to get his or her vibrational level up?

L: They would, but many can't.

B: I thought there was never a lost soul.

L: Not so. There is never a lost soul as long as it is in a human shell. Once it transitions out, that is the beginning of a different vibration.

B: Is it possible for a soul to cease to exist?

L: Sadly enough, energy can be destroyed, and we are all made of energy. It can be changed. It can be reframed or modified.

B: Are there souls who help in the reframing? Essentially, that is their role in spirit?

L: Absolutely.

B: That is consistent with other theories. If I could put a term on your role there, would it be exclusively as a soul guide?

L: [*smiling*] Let's say I'm in the buddy system.

B: Are there other roles or jobs?

L: Yes. Caring for animals, planets. Also, the trees, fire, the earth, and other vibrational properties that you are not aware of. Many, absolutely.

B: Laz, can you give me an idea of what it is like in a day of your life? I know that time does not exist for you, but could you put it in human terms? What would you be doing?

L: Since I have been with you? Humorous. [*laughing*]

Laz seems to take every opportunity to teach me that all things should not be so analytical and serious. I sit and shake my head because I know what is coming—the continuation of his humor, Shirlet's laughter, but also some serious learning.

L: I like Wheaties, but sometimes I'll get Coco Puffs. Let's see…I get up. I put a white robe on…wait, I always have a white robe on. I don't really like sandals, so I go barefoot, and I prefer the beach, so why don't you move? [*everyone is laughing and then much more serious*] Actually, I am one with energy, and energy is one with me. Your vibration is the connection to us at this point, and your vibration allows me to communicate with you. So, putting that into perspective, a day in the life of myself would be to try and fit into your vibration level in order to help you succeed in helping others. It would be an introspective type of life, if you wanted to put a term on it. I am watching, and I am feeling what you feel. I feel your emotions. I feel your pain. I feel your happiness. I feel your love and your loneliness. I feel your connection to this planet and your connection to others. I feel your need to be transmitted into a feeling to be needed again. So really, I guess my day would be the same as your day.

B: And because you are a guide to many souls, you would be feeling that multiple times. Correct?

L: Actually, it would be as if you considered a giant wagon wheel. Consider how the pegs of the wheel go around. Consider that at the end of each peg that I am connected to a soul. Hmm…I really have to be versatile, don't I? [*smiling*] Consider that but multiply by many pegs.

B: Give me an idea how many pegs you are watching over.

L: Thousands.

B: That would be hard for a human to understand, wouldn't it?

L: I have people underneath doing some work. [*smiling*] You are one of them when you are with me. Humans don't realize that their soul is not just a thing to them. Don't you know that when you rest, your soul goes out, and it goes its own way, and it actually guides others? So you would be a lower-vibration guide on this planet for many others. You would be watching over many people right now as I am watching over all of you.

B: Is that an extension of a responsibility I have over there? So that while I am resting here, I put forth some of those responsibilities?

L: Yes. But all humans do.

B: Even humans of a lower-vibration level or even negative vibration?

L: Yes, but those with negative intention are not going to do anything positive. They may be a voice in your head saying to do something unacceptable.

Truthfully, I had a difficult time with much of what Laz had to say—not because of the work I would have to do to elevate my personal vibration level, because I had been getting that from the beginning, but rather that the world of souls could possibly be a place where some who die are so confused that they may feel lost. On the other hand, I was encouraged to learn that there are others who are available to assist in modifying what may be considered negative energy; however, I just couldn't get my head around a soul, either voluntarily or through other means, losing part of its energy identity.

For those of us who aspire to become soul guides upon our return, perhaps we should look into what the benefit package entails because it doesn't seem that Laz and the others get much in the way of vacation time. As for me, it looks like I do a little unpaid moonlighting on the side with Laz during this incarnation, which I was not aware of. I wonder whether he has been purposely withholding that from me for fear I may ask for some form of compensation. Hmm...I'll think more about this.

CHAPTER 24

It's a Pumpkin's Life

Creation and manifestation have always been at the core of what these two soul guides suggest is the purpose of our existence. Numerous times they have queried me on understanding how we all came to be and the importance of continued participation in the formation of life. As a final attempt in designing an exercise to demonstrate the level of importance within the act of creation, Ucerous interjects what appears to be a simple Halloween gesture. I'm more aware, however, of his teaching style, and despite his attempt at humor and disarming me, I recognize that he is formulating his final exam on the expression and seriousness of the design of human life and the role the creator plays.

>Ucerous: I guess I am chopped liver. I haven't been asked any questions yet. Ask me something. I am waiting.

>Bud: OK. With Laz having previously explained a screen-door analogy about dimensions of the spirit world, can I assume that you are not in the same square where Laz resides?

>U: Why would you assume that? [*with levity*] Are you thinking that they are that small that there might not be enough room?

>B: No. [*to Shirlet*] Hey, U said something funny. [*both laughing*]

Shirlet: I think he couldn't resist.

B: I always thought you were a more advanced soul.

U: I might be in the part that holds the screens together. [*smiling*] So you tell me, now I have some questions for you. How will you hold yourself together when your self is wanting to leave this shell because it wants to do something on a different term that is not the term that you wanted to hold yourself together?

I believe that U is referring to private conversations where I disclosed that I had become increasingly interested in their existence and the actuality that my other soul mates existed there. For a time, we had talked about getting more focused on the accomplishments of this incarnation and less on speculative alternatives such as the spirit world.

B: Can I ask you a question first? Is that why I have some thoughts about wanting to return to spirit? Not by harming myself, but wanting to be someplace other than here and with other mates?

U: Yes. It's curiosity. I want you to do something for me.

B: Homework?

U: Yes. It's important homework. Both Laz and I want you to get a pumpkin. I want you to sit it there, and I want you to, for the first twenty-four hours, communicate with it. I want you to see what that pumpkin is thinking. What it is thinking about life? Hmm… now think about this. That pumpkin's life depends on where you set it. That pumpkin's life depends on what you do with it. It has no interaction unless you give it. That pumpkin depends solely on you. Think about that while you are communicating.

B: [*taking a deep breath*] You could almost use anything with this analogy and take it anywhere.

Laz: That is what we are doing. There is a reason that it is a pumpkin. After you have communicated for twenty-four hours, I want you to see what that soul, that essence, in that pumpkin looks like. After you find what it looks like, I want you to put that face on that pumpkin. I want you to be the creator of something. I want you to have a life in your hands that you are responsible for. I want you to create that pumpkin. You are going to watch as that pumpkin grows and gets older and falls apart. You are going to keep talking to it because you need to know its true thoughts. This will answer many questions for you.

B: As to why I feel the need sometimes to separate from here?

U: Absolutely. Depending on where you set the pumpkin.

B: [*to Shirlet*] He knows where I will set it because he knows me.

U: We will see where it goes.

B: [*to Shirlet*] He is conflicting me because what he is saying...my first instinct is to put it in my meditation area. Second thoughts are that it will live longer outside.

L: Hmm...if you were to put it in your meditation room, it may be happy, but it also means it will only see you once in a while. That means it has energy and will never see the outside world. So that would be like putting you in a place with no windows. You would not be able to get out unless someone carried you out. Would that be appropriate?

B: That is why I was initially conflicted. My thoughts are to give the pumpkin the best opportunity to live as long as it can. If I put it inside, which would be convenient to me, its life will be shorter. If outside, it has better chances, but it will be inconvenient to me.

L: Wow! Now you know how the creator felt.

[silence]

B: What you are saying, Laz, is to let those slivers of glass from the beautiful vase go way out there wasn't an easy decision for the creator? There obviously, however, was some intention or truth to allow that to happen.

L: Because you are a pumpkin that wants to experience love. Wants to touch, feel, sense, taste, and see. Why shouldn't you? So to give it the face and stay outside would be so incredible. But then, it is out in the elements. It is cold. It is freezing. It needs help. The bugs are getting to it, invading and attacking it. But it has to be there to be able to learn and to be able to have the sparks of life. To be able to feel again. Then you will know what the creator felt.

B: The pumpkin becomes me?

U: We will see how that goes.

B: [*to Shirlet*] In a simple Halloween story, the pumpkin becomes life.

L: For our creator, if you think about it, despite being all knowing, all seeing, and all energy—that energy has to find itself sad, feeling bad, and maybe not wanting something to happen. But it had to let it all happen for the individual to live. Think about it. People want to know why God doesn't stop all of it, people dying. The pumpkin will teach you a great lesson and a lesson for many others. You determine the soul path of the pumpkin as the creator saw your life progress.

It appears silly, maybe even childish, to look at creation through the eyes of a pumpkin. But to think beyond the simplicity is like looking beyond the written word within a patient chart when assessing the diagnosis and treatment of someone with emotional challenges. There are answers for us in everything that we do, and this tricky piece of homework was sure to end in an explanation of why life extends and retracts through each soul's existence.

I decided to select two small pumpkins. There are many Amish farms near my home, so locating a pumpkin was easy. I chose two, thinking that I preferred that these two pumpkins have a companion as I composed their future life and existence. If I was going to be their guide or the creator of their future, perhaps I could increase the odds of a long life if each pumpkin had a companion.

I find energy connection to be a strange phenomenon, especially during deep meditation. Connecting with nonhuman energy is foreign to me despite previous attempts that were encouraged by Laz and U. As I sat in my meditation room contemplating the seriousness of my guide's request, my doubt increased, but I was determined that if I could find a way to relax and be at ease, perhaps my guides would aid me in connecting with my two new friends.

Laz told me that one can start an energy exchange by asking for a frame of reference or a name, so I approached my meditation from that point of view. Would these two newly picked pumpkins have names? After some time, my mind came upon two, Ellis and Cleave, the larger of the two being Ellis. These were not familiar names, and I wasn't sure that Cleave was even a name. This energy from the fruit called Ellis was not angry but disturbed, or maybe the feeling could be better described as "cheated." I sensed that the premature culling of this fruit from the pumpkin field had taken away the opportunity for the essence of Ellis to become whole. It was as if Ellis's life span had been determined by the farmer with complete disregard for Ellis's expectations. Life for Ellis would forever be limited and apparently unfulfilled, and there was nothing that could be done to correct that. The only other option would be to concentrate on the best life possible, but I wasn't picking that up.

Cleave was a different story. Better stated, he was 180 degrees from Ellis. His circumstances were identical, having been gleaned from the same patch before full maturity. The attitude from this energy, however, was remarkably different. He seemed wide-eyed and energetic, ready to get on with his existence. He loved the fact that he was here and was completely ready to explore all the possibilities within whatever time frame he had.

After some time, I tried to represent the facial expressions of Ellis and Cleave, and in doing so Ellis ended up looking very stern and Cleave extremely joyful. Completing my first task, I now had to decide what to do with them during their stay with me at the farm. If I was in the role of the creator, how should I arrange for their future, if at all? They were pumpkins and had the right to a predictable existence without interference from me or any outside forces. The attitudes that they brought, cheated or enthusiastic, would determine their quality of life regardless of whether they lived outside or within the confines of my shelter. I quickly realized that this was obviously more difficult than just buying two pumpkins.

What did the creator do? Created souls and gave free will to explore, grow, and eventually become one with everything. If the source of all things ruminated about each soul's existence, I could identify with that through the pumpkins. Every part of me would have liked to have protected Ellis and Cleave from the approaching winter elements. Surely that would preserve their outer skin and help them avoid premature disintegration. But in doing so, Ellis would have been further cheated and convinced that his existence was a byproduct of my decisions and those of that Amish farmer and not a responsibility of his own decision making. Cleave was just glad to be here regardless of any limitations placed on him by human interventions.

As I write this, they are still here at the farm, but the weather has turned brutally cold. I suspect that all pumpkins living outside are negatively affected by this turn of events. From time to time, I move Ellis and Cleave to different locations on the farm, hoping that increases the life experience, but I try not to interfere more than that. Having said that, it must be painful for the creator to watch what happens to all of us. Perhaps we are moved from time to time by him or his watchers, the guides, in order to have alternative life experiences and increase our chances of achieving our soul path. In the end, however, it will be our way of behaving that will determine the life we have.

Laz and U were right. This simple pumpkin story spoke volumes to me. The truth of my existence centers on maintaining Cleave's mind-set and avoiding Ellis's. I need to be bright-eyed, honest, and appreciative of the life I have regardless of my circumstances. I intend to fulfill an agreed-upon obligation as a soul choosing to come to this place. That obligation is compromised only by my avoidance and doubt of my core beliefs. I needed to see the faith my pumpkin friend had in his own survival in order to understand the need to be in agreement with my true purpose—to create and live my life.

Conclusion

As I look back on the start of this adventure, I am drawn to the initial perception I had about guides whose purpose was to assist in my journey on earth. Skepticism and distrust were excellent descriptions of my immediate response when I was informed of their presence during my discussions with Shirlet. In the end, however, it was their personal and positive approach that convinced me to document these dialogues. If they knew me as well as they had shown, I tried to imagine how others would feel if they had the same opportunity. In the end I concluded there was something for everyone in what they were conveying and how the teachings were transforming my beliefs and perhaps that might assist others.

Yes, I can honestly say I was completely unprepared for this undertaking. Looking back, I believed these conferences would give me some insight yet continue to allow me to conduct my life in a manner that protected who I was and what I had become. Arriving at the truth, I learned, came at an enormous spiritual price when faced with the way I had lived my life. Fortunately, the freedom that came to me once I faced the reality of certain life situations outweighed any spiritual delay or the cost I may have experienced. And what was that cost? The loss of life's focus, energy, and special relationships, but more importantly the loss of time to complete my path. I am sure that there is more soul learning to come because my journey with Laz and U continues as I write.

My closest friend surprised me when he indicated that my association with Laz and Ucerous had allowed him to review his lifelong agnostic beliefs. He was taken by the stories and advice offered in both the dialogues and in the homework assignments. Over time we reviewed the tapes together and talked about them constantly. We both understood that the lessons were strikingly consistent, positive, and helpful for anyone regardless of the source or any doubt either of us have about spiritual matters. After all, Laz and U's focus is about what we hope for, what we trust, and what we believe.

In my early transformative education, I have discovered that there are core values and objectives to continually strive for, including those initially recommended by "You can call me John": truth, honesty, and humility. Life will teach us these, he would say, one way or another. Unfortunately I chose the more difficult learning path and in doing so wasted an enormous amount of time and unfortunately the soul energy of others.

I have understood that truth comes with compassion. Without it, any one of us can confuse our attempts to reach for the truth and mistakenly inflict cruelty. As Laz suggested, authenticated truth always hurts, but that distress comes from an individual's internal examination of his or her actions, not from external recommendations by others.

Further there is the soul's principal value of creation. I no longer wonder what my intention is on this day because I embrace the obligation to participate in the ongoing creation within me and about me. Without this I am not carrying my weight, and I am not constructively involved in assisting those around me. My father would tell me that our responsibility was to leave this place better than we found it. Well, Laz gives the same simple advice but with perhaps a deeper and more soulful meaning.

The key intention of my soul guides is to assist in my life journey and provide possible alternative selections as I attempt to meet the challenges of this place. Throughout my exchanges with all of these guides, I have found a consistency in their use of the number three whenever I requested general advice for living. As an example, when asking for a blueprint for a successful existence, guides suggested three concepts: First, there is no time for uncertainty or doubt. I am convinced that this may have been specifically developed for me by any number of the guides, but Laz proposed that doubt was more than just my middle name. On a larger scale, uncertainty, he suggested, creates havoc for all of us; and it certainly did for me. Once distrust enters my mind, the primary thoughts I have seem to disintegrate. Jesus walked on water, they say, because he had no doubt. My mind has the potential to create anything if I eliminate misgivings. Removing doubt has been the most difficult lesson of all for me, and I believe the guides understood that from the beginning, thus their continued emphasis.

Second, Laz intimated that homework and storytelling were intentional and constructed so as to break my learning patterns down to the most basic components. When they communicated through compelling stories, I could not argue with the messages. Further, I was better able to understand that life guidance does not have to be the high-level, analytical, and introspective process I was used to. It can be as modest as giving the thought intention of a rose or the outcome of dropping a playing card. And finally, there is the conviction of believing in myself and that I am truly a blessed soul. Both Laz and U never wavered from that premise. From the outset both guides understood and emphasized that anything was possible for me, including the writing of this material.

Interlaced in the dialogues was one essential tenet which was that there is no hope without faith. I was to learn from those discussions and subsequent analyses that truth, growth, and the fulfillment of a soul path require the combined effort of both and that my living place was becoming void of the essential resources to have hope and faith flourish. There is accuracy in a comment made by a Thai monk prior to my leaving the Virginia monastery to the effect that the healers of this world need to fully and completely understand tragedy; only then he would say we were on our way to instilling hope. The question for me remains: Am I capable of encouraging and developing the necessary hope and faith to move beyond any of life's misfortunes?

One phrase that resonates with me is "Think about it." I find myself in consultation meetings ruminating about this saying, hoping I do not embarrass my client by blurting it out. That did not stop Laz, however, from finding his teaching moments on the subject. He was relentless on the topic of free will and its impact on our lifetimes and the lives of those we love. Nowhere was that clearer than in his emphasis that I understand and respect the soul path of all individuals. Adjust your expectations of those you encounter, he would assert, and everyone will be better for it. All you need to do is think about it.

I can remember my mother indicating to us as small children that life would be just wonderful if we would do everything she requested when she requested it. That wasn't the case then, nor is it the case now. The guides taught me to concentrate on my own evolution and growth path, not the deviation of another's direction. Both guides explained that redirecting someone to a path that is more desirable from my perspective would not make me whole. I cannot give up my path to appease another. Further, it is disrespectful to impose my preference on another soul. As humans, Laz would say, we are incapable of accurately discerning what is appropriate for another's soul journey.

Kadecious once challenged me by asking if the tears of the clinicians working with me burned or healed the children at a facility where I had provided consultative services. I understood that to mean this: Are the clinicians working with the children providing what is truly necessary for healing, or are they interacting with the children because it makes the clinicians feel better? We like to intervene and assist others, and there are many times when our actions are appropriate. It makes us feel good. But if we forcefully insert our beliefs into another's soul plan, that is a different act. We should pause at those moments because if our recommendations cause a diversion we will be the one judged on the outcome of that decision process.

My systematic path through life could not have been more disrupted than when Laz and U repeatedly verbalized that all thought creates solid form and that I create my own reality. I so much wanted to blame everything on something outside myself; plus, I had advanced avoiding all responsibility to the level of an art form and was disturbed that this teaching brought me solidly back to earth. I would not be the first person to avoid my life's responsibilities, but now, under the watchful eyes of Laz and U, there is little chance of that happening.

Discovering that I can transform events when I change my own perception of people and places opened up a myriad of possibilities. I remember Laz asking me to go back to a time in a delicate relationship in Maryland and change the outcome. As a spiritual novice, I considered all the possible methods of returning to a time I was trying to forget. Laz laughed, telling me I had to change my mind about what had transpired and the way in which I had catalogued the relationship outcomes, not try to physically manifest a method of returning to a past time. He suggested that while living in the past can be toxic, the control over whether I stay or leave that setting is solely my own. My Thai monk friends earlier echoed that by referring to any decision to stay in the past was my self-imposed suffering. Laz simply reframed their teaching.

Reassessing the controlling and analytical approach I had toward life made me more realistic about my interactions with others and opened my eyes to an architect's view on my change process. In doing so I was allowing myself to build a solid soul path dream one brick at a time. As Ucerous suggests, attuning yourself and your vibration gives you the possibility to create something different in your life. The net result? It's free will. Free to be whatever you can imagine. Free to be open to the likelihood that what you can envision can become real.

Throughout my time with these two guides, I have consistently tried to learn as much as I could about topics that were outside their agenda—my soul path growth. I am sure they know by now that my curiosity will lead me to ask more about the functions of energy, the universe, and why there is always a possibility that soul energy can be so modified as to change the original intention. I find myself needing more of an explanation as to why a spirit would have such a process. They have used the word *modification*, but to me the ability to alter energy underscores the real possibility that the essence of what makes up a soul can be altered. I remain curious about this phenomenon and intend on revisiting the topic in the future.

Another question that occupies my mind is the guides' concern over the actions of humankind and the countless possibilities that might result from our behavior. This is a region of many possibilities and potentially vibrant discussion. It is also an area that falls well outside the realm of a soul guide's responsibilities. As they discussed very early on, their intention is my soul growth, not to make predictions about the future for me or anyone else. The guide Ucerous wouldn't touch those topics, and Laz shut down almost immediately after briefly discussing my possible role in the future, indicating that too much information could transform my growth.

One observation I became aware of during a more private discussion about people and relationships was the impact of time and the choices others make. As an example, Laz shared with me that if he gave me any information about an individual and how he or she could impact my life, any change in that individual would amend the outcome. I understood that to mean that if everything stayed the same, I could expect his observation to occur, but that even the simplest change would revise the expected event. Free will, he said, affects everything. Maybe that is why the guides avoid becoming psychics in matters of the future and leave that to earthly oracles like Shirlet. I once joked that it is like being Jimmy the Greek, trying to determine the over/under of an event and knowing you can only account for so many of the variables. Despite this, I remain curious about the path we as a human race are creating and what will happen to us.

Additionally, there is the issue of the light and my soul guides' place within the path of that light. I was taken aback when Laz shared his place and his focus. I had a picture in my mind of the space he occupies and how he operates within it. It was more like what we might be accustomed to here in a human-shell form. After all, he indicated that we have been together there. So I assumed something and imagined wrong.

I learned two important things through the sharing of his space and the nature of his soul. I know, without hesitation, that I am seeing things about his existence, as he says, with a child's eyes. The magnitude and totality of my soul truth and existence are not in my realm of understanding or my vibration level, and it is likely to stay as long as I am in this place. This is not meant to be demeaning; it is just a fact of being human.

Further, the intention of the creator may be far more complex than my understanding of religious dogma. The idea of existing in knowledge of love not based on fear, and the knowledge of kindness and empathy not based on sorrow, brings a warmth to my heart. Laz brought me back to the basics during that session when he explained that the light (God) is forgiveness, kindness, perception, birth, and all that is known. It made me remember that I am here for a purpose and that my obligation is to find and fulfill that objective, not simply to find a way to get through the day. Like Ellis and Cleave, how I go about achieving all of this is on me, but in the end, if I do not satisfy my intended soul path, it will not be the fault of the time Laz and Ucerous have spent with me. Like all soul guides, they are available to assist; the responsibility and work are for me alone.

There was one final concern I had in relation to the reception of what I had learned about soul guides. There is the issue of this six-year exploration as a "channeling" event. I had a lot of difficulty with this

CONCLUSION

from the beginning, and I was very reluctant to share these experiences with anyone but my closest friends. Further complicating this issue is the fact that mainstream publishers tend to have a negative attitude about spirit-guide communication and so typically exclude such literature from their lists. This would surely prohibit me from "getting the message out there" as Laz recommended.

Regardless, I reviewed channeling writing and noticed a wide variety of approaches, everything from counsel to the masses about recommendations from spirits to universal consciousness advising on similar lessons. In the end, I took my predicament to Laz and U to see what they would say about my increasing conflict. After all, our interactions were almost exclusively related to personal matters. In that final session, their responses were interesting and insightful. Essentially they spoke of us as humans having the capacity to grow and communicate and that within that we channel every day and in everything we do. When we go to our churches to pray, we are actually channeling our conception of God. When we are asking for our brothers and sisters who have died to hear what we are saying, that is channeling. When we think about our beloved pet that has passed, we are channeling. That voice in your head can be your people connecting with you. It is such a sad thing, Laz remarked, that people don't trust channeling because they do it every day. He found it quite disturbing that anyone would not believe in something everyone was doing. He referred to it as being hypocritical and said that no one should follow that path and cut off that communication.

From my initial connection with Laz and U, the primary intention has been to disclose that soul guides exist, are available to assist us and continually try to connect with us through diverse means. Yet, as you have read, my six year association with these energies has formed so much more.

During my last visit with Laz he used the word karma for the first time in describing the lessons learned from the first six years of our relationship and the writing of this material. He implied that karma was a process of determining significant causality through introspective self learning. Confused about his intent I requested that he be specific. He said, "For years you have devoted your existence to getting into the heads of others…now all will have the opportunity to get into yours. What do you think they will learn? Tell me your true karma lesson and how that wisdom has the potential to save a life?"

Moving from the purpose of the hazy window to the exploration of my authentic truth and soul path, not once have I considered my objective to be specifically about saving lives. After all, I was consumed in soul guide lessons and doing my best to incorporate the results into my daily life.

In the end my karma lesson concentrated on comments Laz expressed years ago. He revealed that somewhere in my existence is the private need to know that I am *truly loved* regardless of my life experiences. Guides exist, he suggested, to insure that we know true affection and recognize that in creation of our existence *no one is ever alone*. I believe understanding we are never abandoned in this lifetime and that we are treasured has the power to save lives.

As a final thought, I often consider and marvel at the possibility of others finding the methods and courage to connect with the souls that guide us. If that occurs, my prying imagination explodes with the possibilities of the life altering karma lessons that can be imparted and as a result the likely lives that can be saved. I for one believe it is a worthy and courageous path worth traveling. *Think about it...* because all you need to do is listen.

Topics from Kadecious

Kadecious was the first higher guide who came to me on multiple occasions, and I am not completely sure what this complex guide's role was in my life. Many times he asked me spontaneous questions that did not directly relate to the topic at hand. They were thought provoking, to say the least, and although I gave my best effort in trying to answer each one, the ultimate answers, he would say, reside in each of us. I offer a few for you to meditate upon. I wish you all good fortune in the discovery of your personal solutions.

1. Can you show me a color that you haven't seen in seven days?
2. John once said, "You cannot control those who desire to control you."
3. Just are those who conform to a rumor that was started from within.
4. Can you control the weather? If you can, can you control a soul that has lost its way? And could you heal it if it was a thousand miles away?
5. Tough is the nail that can penetrate wood as a solid source, but it cannot penetrate air. Why?
6. You have pores in your body, yet you hold water. Why can't you hold it in your hand?
7. A protocol would be a device that would be used to control the masses, but the masses could never control the device.

8. Stifle those who came to the sand's edge and never sunk down an inch for the knowledge.
9. For all clinicians: If I am a client of yours, and I come with a flesh wound, will your tears heal it or burn it?
10. Can you change a sentence before it is invented?

Acknowledgments

I am deeply thankful for the devotion and support of my daughter, Case, without whom I never would have started this journey. She has been the inspiration behind my visitations to Wat Yarnna Rangsee and my continual pursuit of life's spiritual answers.

I would like to thank Shirlet Enama for taking on the project of working with me on my soul adventure, this writing project, and for suggesting that it remain a reality-based soul discussion. Special thanks to my favorite human, Ralph Morini, for his undying assistance, his belief in my first-time efforts, and his acceptance of my personal transformation and to his wife Diane Morini who initiated all of my unconventional learning and took on the role of a conduit to the world of guides; thanks also to my artist brother, Jim Megargee, who supplied creative input, acceptance, and critique when needed; to my good friend Vivian Macklin, who assisted in early editorial efforts and provided both photographs and validation of my voyage; and to Susan Kemper and her daughter, Alyssa, who, over tacos, appeared at just the right time to gently stimulate my acceptance of unconventional paths. A very special thanks to all who provided publishing assistance, including Melissa and Lauren from the CS professional editing group as well as staff involved in the formatting and creative decision making.

Thanks to all those who read early editions without judgment, my very good supporter Michelle Williams for all her energy and personal connection, the Barnes & Noble bookstores in Exton and Devon, Pennsylvania, for unknowingly providing writing space and the energy of all the authors residing on the tables and shelves, and to the woman in Maryland who, without knowing it, drove me to examine the answers about the truth of my existence.

My heartfelt appreciation to all the Taiwanese monks for their patience and support. My sincere indebtedness to all the guides for their love and direct input into this writing, including Elias, "You can call me John," Hamlin, and Kadecious. And for a second time, very special gratitude to Laz and U.

About the Author

Bud Megargee is the founder and CEO of Megargee Healthcare Group, located in the beautiful, green, horse country of Southeastern Pennsylvania. He holds advanced degrees in health care and the psychoeducational process, and he has been both a practicing clinician and a senior health care executive specializing in behavioral health for over forty years. His focus on transformation, medical integration, and contemplative psychology has sent him on an unconventional path to incorporate Eastern philosophies in the treatment of emotional challenges in hospital and community mental health settings throughout the United States.

Megargee lives with his daughter, Case. Both are avid runners and supporters of various causes for the homeless.

Bud Megargee can be reached at www.budmegargee.com

Made in the USA
Middletown, DE
08 June 2015